the old pond—
a frog jumps in:
the sound of water
　　　　—Bashō

Haiku Moment

An Anthology of Contemporary North American Haiku

Edited by Bruce Ross

TUTTLE PUBLISHING
Tokyo • Rutland, Vermont • Singapore

To my Mother, Esther Spector Ross

Published by Tuttle Publishing, an imprint of Periplus Editions (HK) Ltd., with editorial offices at 364 Innovation Drive, North Clarendon, Vermont 05759 U.S.A.

Library of Congress Control Number: 93-60220

ISBN-10: 0-8048-1820-7
ISBN-13: 978-0-8048-1820-9

Distributed by:

North America, Latin America & Europe
Tuttle Publishing
364 Innovation Drive
North Clarendon, VT 05759-9436 U.S.A.
Tel: 1 (802) 773-8930
Fax: 1 (802) 773-6993
info@tuttlepublishing.com
www.tuttlepublishing.com

Asia Pacific
Berkeley Books Pte. Ltd.
130 Joo Seng Road #06-01
Singapore 368357
Tel: (65) 6280-1330
Fax: (65) 6280-6290
inquiries@periplus.com.sg
www.periplus.com

10 09 08 07   10 9 8 7 6 5
Printed in Singapore
Cover design by Greta D. Sibley

ACKNOWLEDGMENTS

I would like to acknowledge the assistance and advice, or offered assistance and advice, provided at various stages in the production of this anthology by the following people: L. A. Davidson, Doris Heitmeyer, William J. Higginson, Marshall Hryciuk, Elizabeth Searle Lamb, Minna Lerman, Francine Porad, Jane Reichhold, Keith Southward, Robert Spiess, Ruby Spriggs, George Swede, Rysai Takeshita, Sue Stapleton Tkach, and John Wills. I would also like to acknowledge my appreciation of the good wishes afforded to me by many of the haiku poets in this volume. Special thanks are due to Dorothy Howard, the most tolerant of hostesses, Cor van den Heuvel, for a grand tour of New York, Linda Licklider Smith, an editor with a sense of humor, and Murray David Ross, creator of the *sumi* paintings adorning *Haiku Moment*.

A NOTE ON THE POEMS

The vast majority of the haiku chosen for this anthology were originally written or published between 1982 and 1992. A most obvious exception would be some of Nick Virgilio's haiku, collected in his *Selected Haiku* (1985) but written many years before the 1982 cutoff date. All of the haiku in this anthology were composed in English; thus, many fine French Canadian, Mexican, and Japanese-American haiku were not included. Most of the haiku in this collection are nature poems, some of these merely nature sketches overlaid with recognizable human emotion. When human nature is directly represented, it is almost always subsumed under or correlated to some element of non-human nature. In general, these haiku are meant to reflect either the style of the Bashō School of haiku with its emphasis on the presentation of temporal loneliness and emotional objectivity in the treatment of nature subjects (and occasionally, as in later Bashō, an elevated warm-heartedness found in one's relation to commonplace things) or the haiku of Issa with their joyful evocations of the liveliness and empathic resonance found in the natural world. All of the haiku in this anthology, moreover, should convey a moment of insight experienced by a poet in real time through real beings and objects, a moment that the reader may enter and share.

INTRODUCTION

Perhaps the two most well-known haiku in contemporary Japan were composed respectively by the Japanese haiku poets Basho and Issa.[1] Basho's poem is the most recognized haiku in the world:

furuike ya	the old pond—
kawazu tobikomu	a frog jumps in:
mizu no oto	the sound of water

Issa's haiku is:

suzume no ko	sparrow's child
soko noke soko noke	out of the way, out of the way!
o-uma ga toru	the stallion's coming through

What links the two haiku is a particular mode of attention directed toward nature. Each poet wants to participate in the life of non-human nature, but their poems convey this desire through different kinds of emotion. Basho maintains a somber meditative openness to nature that allows him to be objective about his subject. His haiku is moreover a metaphysical rather than an aesthetic exercise. This haiku is meant to reveal spiritual reality. The frog's splash reverberates with the Zen Buddhist idea that *nirvana*, transcendence, is found within *samsara*, the perceived world, and that this realization can take place instantaneously. The realization is evoked in the relation of the stillness of the old pond and the brief motion and sound of the frog's jump. The poet's consciousness has completely merged with the pond's reality as stillness and the frog's reality as movement and sound in a state of no-mind or deep awareness that may provoke a Zennian spiritual awakening.[2] Issa, on the other hand, engages his subjects with child-like energetic spontaneity in what has been called a "mood of natural faith."[3] His sparrow haiku is a testament to this belief in an uncorrupted world of nature in which each being is spiritually animated. In this world there is a democracy of human and non-human life so that Issa may warn (or wish to warn) the young sparrow of the incipient danger coming his way. Like a good Buddhist, Issa respects the sanctity of all life forms. And like a good Shintoist, he is sympathetic toward the spirit or *kami* in natural beings. Thus his haiku reveals the vital spiritual essences of his sparrow and his stallion within the context of this somehow familiar, yet fairy tale-like, dramatic event. In Issa's haiku, the non-human beings display human emotions; thus, the sparrow in this haiku is someone's child who has to be looked out for. Issa personalized nature. Bashō objectified it. Bashō's attention toward nature is based on silence. Issa's attention toward nature is based on his impassioned sense of his brotherhood with all living things.

The movement from a special attention toward non-human nature to some kind of union with that nature is a central facet of Japanese culture and is derived from Taoism, Buddhism, and Shintoism. This movement from attention to union at the heart of the haiku tradition is for the most part alien to Western culture. This point was recently addressed by Sonō Uchida, President of the Haiku International Association:

> Haiku has also developed as a poem which expresses deep feelings for nature, including human beings. This follows the traditional Japanese idea that man is part of the natural world, and should live in harmony with it. This differs considerably from the Western way of thinking, in which man is regarded as being independent of, and perhaps superior to, the rest of nature.[4]

To somewhat clarify this divergence, we should note that in the long poetic traditions of both the East and the West the exploration of man's relation to nature is predominant. Broadly speaking, the poetics of the East reflects an ontological union of man's consciousness with nature in which nature is of equal valence to man while the poetics of the West reflects an allegorical subsuming of nature in which man dominates nature. Eastern and Western concepts of subjectivity thus differ, the East accenting an emotional relation of the self to nature and the West accenting an intellectual relation to nature. In the East nature tends to dominate consciousness. In the West the mind tends to determine consciousness. Thus one great impediment stands in the way of Western attempts at haiku.

Nonetheless, haiku has been attempted in most of the major languages of the world, perhaps because despite its brevity as possibly the shortest lyric poem, haiku displays a concentrated allusiveness through its idiom of concrete nature images that transfers some of the spiritual presence of nature that is evoked in the poetics of the East.

Traditional Japanese poetry is based on combinations of lines of five and seven *onji*, a syllable-like unit of a vowel or a consonant and vowel. Haiku uses a pattern of five-seven-five *onji* originally arranged in vertical columns. A haiku in Japanese is extremely short so that it is recited in one breath. Since an average syllable in English is much longer than an *onji*, modern haiku in English generally range from twelve to fourteen syllables, although many haiku poets try to maintain a five-seven-five syllable count. Some modern English haiku use the three-liner vertical column arrangement, but horizontal one-liners, two-liners, and four-liners occur, with the horizontal three-liner short-long-short construction the most common one. English haiku tends also to lack some of the sound color of their Japanese counterparts because the prevalence of vowels in Japanese words and the frequent use of assonance, alliteration, and other sound values in Japanese haiku have not been sufficiently recognized by the non-Japanese world as indigenous to the haiku form.

Japanese haiku also uses *kireji* ("cutting words"), particles of language that indicate a pause or a stop. *Kireji* usually separate discrete image clusters and often coincide with the short-long-short line breaks in haiku. English haiku normally uses punctuation marks in much the same way. Traditional Japanese haiku also includes either a *kigo* ("season word") or a *kidai* ("seasonal topic"). These words as one, two, or even three images provide the emotional focus in a haiku. They are associated in the Japanese mind with conventional images particularly connected to one of the four seasons or the New Year's month, setting up allusions that do not translate well into the world of English-language haiku. The vast cultural and climatic differences of the non-Japanese world prevents this. Modern English haiku is therefore not formally dependent upon a standardized season word. The concrete manner in which Japanese haiku presents its nature images is however easily adopted by other cultures. These images appeal directly to the senses without the intervention of abstraction or commentary and, for the most part, without figurative language, a remarkable alternative to the Western poetic tradition of moral verse, standardized figurative expression, and symbolic images. The Japanese nature image conveys real experience. It is objective in that the image itself is normally not overdetermined by the poet's subjective or imaginative self, a common feature of the poetics of the West. The Japanese image also occurs in the present tense, highlighting haiku's emphasis upon real lived experience. When personal memories or allusions to Japanese culture or literature enter a haiku, they are relegated to or associated with a given present tense image occurring in a particular instance of time.

Further, each of these particular instances of time is intended to present an insight into reality, often evoking moments of transcendence, awe, or simply the joy found in the unexpected. Underlying this emphasis on the given moment of time is the Buddhist idea that the world is made anew in each moment. A kind of divine spontaneity thus inheres in each moment. Robert Spiess, editor of *Modern Haiku*, describes the significance of haiku in relation to this cosmic dimension of the moment: "The whole of life is in each moment, not in the past, not in the future—and thus a true haiku is vitally important because it is a moment of total and genuine awareness of the reality of the Now."[5] A haiku does not simply portray mere nature. It reveals the universal importance of each particular in nature as it burgeons forth and relates to other particulars in a given moment.

Traditional Japanese haiku has four recognized masters. Matsuo Bashō (1644-94) may be credited with establishing the haiku form. He did this by first allowing *renga*, the conventional linked poetic form of one hundred stanzas, to incorporate less artistically decorous subject matter, thus opening *renga* to a more comprehensive representation of experience as the renamed *haikai*. Secondly, and more importantly, he separated as a discrete unit the *hokku*, the opening three-lined five-seven-five *onji* stanza of linked forms, from the *haikai* sequence.[6] The presiding elements of the *hokku* up to Bashō's time had been its inclusion of a reference to the seasons and a concluding *kireji*. Bashō thus transformed the *hokku* into something resembling haiku by highlighting the nature imagery represented at the moment of composition and by eliminating the *kireji* as a mandatory end element. The *hokku* thus became a self-contained moment of felt experience. Bashō's poetics moreover turned this new kind of poetry into a serious form of literature by using it to address in the deepest manner the relation of consciousness to nature as objectively represented, charged moments of real experience. Yosa Buson (1716-83), the next great developer of the haiku form, emphasized the universal nature of the subject matter of haiku by focusing upon human as well as nature subjects. Buson also altered the aesthetic nature of haiku by highlighting subjective or imaginative expression and by treating haiku images in a painterly-like style.

Kobayashi Issa (1763-1827) introduced an idiosyncratic element into haiku through his child-like identification with nature and human behavior, often depicting a lowly or subjugated person or thing in colloquial language. The expressed heart-felt simplicity in Issa's haiku provided common man with an accessible kind of poetic experience. Masaoka Shiki (1867-1902) is the first modern Japanese haiku poet. He is credited with popularizing the term "haiku," a compression of *haikai no ku* ("verse of a linked poem"), as a form completely independent from linked poetry. He favored Buson's "objective" treatment of haiku subjects over Bashō's "airy" spirituality. His own manner of exploring a poetic subject introduces a decidedly modern tone of wit and mental play into haiku.

Since the time of Shiki, the Japanese haiku has undergone numerous stages of development through experiments with many of the common modern directions in poetry and thought.[7] However, the history of Japanese haiku, with a major exception in the earthy haiku of Issa, reflects a poetics that vacillates between a Bashō-like fusion with nature and a Buson-like aesthetic handling of experience, with Bashō's haiku revered more than Buson's, but Buson's style of haiku dominating actual practice. Bashō nonetheless sets the standard for haiku as a metaphysical rather than as an aesthetic exercise.

Although American and non-Japanese haiku poets cannot really produce classical Japanese haiku in the strictest sense because that haiku is determined by codifications of sentiment, ideology, symbol, and intertextual allusion as well as sound values specific to Japanese culture and Japanese haiku, successful versions of haiku in the classic mode have been composed in English and other languages.

The history of North American English-language haiku may be viewed as a continuous unresolved exploration of the objective and subjective qualities of the poetic image. This history can be divided into four stages.[8] The first stage begins during the teens and twenties and continues into the thirties and forties of this century. In 1913, Ezra Pound's manifesto on Imagism argued that poetry must address its subject forthrightly, whether subjectively or objectively, in order to distance itself from nineteenth-century conventions of sentimentality and clichéd figurative expression. His definition of poetry as "an intellectual and emotional complex in an instant of time" redefined poetry as a mental union of imagination, emotion, and perceived external reality. Pound's well-known and most haiku-like poem, the two-liner "In a Station of the Metro," is clearly an exercise in fabricated metaphor. The poem is true to the manifesto of Imagism but not really a haiku, which demands, for one thing, objectively real images. Pound's attempts at haiku-like poems have only family resemblances to haiku, as do those of John Gould Fletcher, Amy Lowell, and other Imagists, and are based upon Pound's response to oriental pictorialism. Nonetheless, Pound and Imagism introduced a more emotionally charged, sophisticated, and accurately depicted image into American poetry.

William Carlos Williams and Objectivism, an extension of Imagism, insisted that American poetry focus on the inner reality of the object, as in the treatment of the objects in his well-known poem "The Red Wheel Barrow" upon which "so much depends."[9] This haiku-like poem quietly evokes a poetics of the objectively present image by accenting apparently ordinary subjects. Williams assumes that consciousness is of the same nature as the external world and that therefore the poet may faithfully perceive, even enter, objective reality. Williams views human imagination as a mechanism that is activated by its encounter with reality itself. As he declares in *Patterson*: "no ideas but in things." For Williams reality presides over poetry and the imagination. Wallace Stevens, on the other hand, showed how American poetry might focus on the inner reality of the subject, as he does in the first line of his Imagist portrait of winter, "The Snow Man": "One must have a mind of winter. . . " The poem's stark emotional coloring and its emphasis on the mental experience of nothingness echoes the Zen Buddhist concept of "no-mind," a desired higher-than-ordinary state of consciousness. Though comprised of mental images, the first of the very haiku-like three-liner stanzas of his "Thirteen Ways of Looking at a Blackbird" likewise captures very closely the subjective, often cheerless, Zennian treatment of haiku images in its depiction of an absolute winter stillness that is deepened by the movement of a blackbird's eye. Opposed to Williams' revelatory realism, Stevens' poetics of the "supreme fiction" holds that the imagination is an aesthetic order imposed upon things. His poems are about reality but not of it, a reflection of the Modernist's turn from the Romantics' direct engagement with nature itself. Williams thus glancingly resembles Bashō in his direct engagement with nature, and Stevens in a like manner resembles Buson in his imaginative rendering of experience. This redefinition of the American haiku was also supported by the publication in the early thirties of Harold Henderson's translations of and introduction to Japanese haiku, *The Bamboo Broom*. Overall, however, the first generation of American haiku-like poetry can be characterized as a poetic overdetermination of the subjectively presented image.

Gary Snyder, Alan Ginsberg, and Jack Kerouac represent the second important stage of the American reception of haiku which centered on the so-called Beat Movement of the fifties. In reaction to the cerebral academic poetry that dominated this period, their haiku and other poetry focused upon the emotional vividness of the subjectively felt present moment. Snyder applied oriental aesthetics to produce poems that evoke the beauty and wildness of nature. Ginsberg used oriental modes and a Romantic sensibility to create Blake-like poems on nature, love, and social criticism and haiku reflecting the unrefined nature of the Beat Movement. Kerouac wrote fiction that explored his own melding of Christian and Buddhist spirituality and strong haiku that breached the moodiness of classical Japanese haiku. In a passage from one of his novels, Kerouac's narrator muses over the Japanese haiku poets who, according to him, grasp experience like children "without literary devices or fanciness of expression." Then, to continue these thoughts of the narrator, a character in the novel who is modeled on Gary Snyder begins to discuss haiku: "'A real haiku's gotta be as simple as porridge and yet make you see the real thing . . . '"[10] Although unsophisticated, these explanations of haiku consider the two major elements of haiku composition: a subjective receptivity to external reality, here described as the emotional spontaneity of children, and an objective presentation of natural images that connect you with "the real thing." That the narrator misses the essentially moody nature of classic Japanese haiku is characteristic of the well-meaning but often misguided reception of haiku by American poets. Snyder is, contrariwise, well versed in Japanese poetics, and his character is almost literally quoting Bashō on the effect that haiku should have on the reader or listener. The Beats centered their understanding of haiku on discussions of Zen Buddhism in the work of D. T. Suzuki and Alan Watts and on the four-volume translation of Japanese haiku begun in nineteen forty-nine by R. H. Blyth. Donald Keene's *Anthology of Japanese Literature* (1955) and the Japanese study in English *Haikai and Haiku* (1958) also helped clarify the nature of haiku during this period. But the Beats' uncritical understanding of Zen and their commitment to passionately lived experience led to the second generation of American haiku poets' over-determination of the subjectively felt external moment.

The third generation of American haiku poets dates from the late fifties and early sixties with English-language introductions to haiku by Kenneth Yasuda (1957) and Harold G. Henderson (1958) and with the establishment of English-language haiku journals beginning with *American Haiku* (1963) and later including *Haiku Highlights* (1965), *Haiku* (1967), *Haiku West* (1967), *Modern Haiku* (1969), *Dragonfly* (1973), *Cicada* (1977), and *Frogpond* (1978). A watershed for this generation is Cor van den Heuvel's pioneering *The Haiku Anthology* (1974), which collected the haiku and theories of haiku of the contemporary American and Canadian haiku poets of the time. It was followed by the equally significant *Canadian Haiku Anthology* (1979) which was edited by George Swede. Important studies of this period, such as Eric Amann's *The Wordless Poem* (1969), Makoto Ueda's *Matsuo Bashō* (1970), and Robert Aitken's *A Zen Wave, Bashō's Haiku and Zen* (1978), examined the relation of classic Japanese haiku to Zen Buddhism. Gary L. Brower provided an important bibliographical resource for the study of haiku in English in his *Haiku in Western Languages* (1972). The haiku poets of *The Haiku Anthology* have a greater knowledge of oriental literature and poetics than the preceding two generations of American haiku poets. And, beyond formal authenticity, aspire to the aesthetic and spiritual underpinnings of Bashō's haiku. The third generation of American haiku poets begin to clarify their Williams-like perception of the inner nature of external images. They also develop subjectively perceived experience to emphasize the Zen-like mental climate of Wallace Stevens' "supreme fiction," as in this haiku by Nick Virgilio:

Lily:
out of the water . . .
out of itself.

Finally, they evoke cosmic revelations about external and internal reality that, for Bashō, are expressed in Buddhist terms and that, for them, are expressed as a transcendence of the normal self and of the normal perception of objects, in a representation of what the contemporary Canadian haiku poet George Swede calls "the unity of nature."[11]

The poets of *The Haiku Anthology* are aware of redefining poetic consciousness: James William Hackett describes haiku's "emphasis upon moment and selfless devotion to suchness (nature just as it is)" by adopting the Buddhist concept *muga* or self-lessness,[12] and Ron Seitz identifies the haiku poet's ego as "no 'I'/ anonymous."[13] They are also aware that they are trying to represent metaphysical reality: Cor van den Heuvel characterizes haiku as having "words [that] become an ontological presence offering a glimpse of the infinite,"[14] and Anita Virgil asserts that haiku demonstrates the "nature of all things of this world: their unique identity and yet their sameness, their evanescence and their eternal quality."[15] Some of the poems in *The Haiku Anthology* through their union of an egoless subject and a metaphysically perceived object produce the emotionally austere classic haiku moment, like this one by Nick Virgilio:

Autumn twilight:
the wreath on the door
lifts in the wind.

A good number of the poems in *The Haiku Anthology*, however, are somewhat overdetermined exercises in artfulness, sentimentality, formal experimentation, nature portraiture, irony, Zen presence, and commentary. The poets of *The Haiku Anthology* and of the third generation of American haiku poets have nonetheless produced pioneering volumes of significant haiku poetry, including those by Matsuo Allard, C. M. Buckaway, Betty Drevniok, James

William Hackett, Michael McClintock, Claire Pratt, O. Mabson Southard, Robert Spiess, George Swede, Cor van den Heuvel, Anita Virgil, and others. This third generation of American haiku poets needs, however, to clarify its perceptions of natural images and to develop an intensity of feeling uncharacteristic of Western sensibility and represented in aesthetic concepts like *aware, yugen, wabi, sabi,* and *karumi* that are associated with classic Japanese haiku and that generally refer to states of mystery and loneliness evoked by nature and humanity which elicit one's emotion. Robert Spiess had similarly expressed a need for English-language haiku to adopt Japanese-like modes of poetic consciousness and haiku-like treatments of experience in his statement of poetics for *The Haiku Anthology*:

> [English-language haiku is] singular in that in using the resources and genius of our language and aspects of our poetics to re-create the haiku moment with words and silence, it also requires the Japanese haiku's disciplined orientation toward heightened awareness, direct perception, immediacy and brevity, suggestion and indirection but nonetheless concreteness and particulariza-tion, poetic naturalness . . . [16]

However the tendency in the fourth generation of American haiku poets of the late seventies, eighties, and early nineties is, unfortunately, to frequently offer catchy moments of sensibility that often rely on obvious metaphoric figures. These American poets desire to create "haiku moments." But a subjective ego, call it sentiment or call it imagination, intrudes upon their perception of the object, creating haiku determined by ironic Imagism.

Individual contemporary American haiku poets are, nonetheless, producing classic haiku moments, some consistently, as for example Lee Gurga in a haiku like this:

> spot of sunlight—
> on a blade of grass the dragonfly
> changes its grip

And some of these haiku poets as well as recent critics of the form have been able to articulate the poetics of modern English haiku. Thus John Beer suggests that the haiku poet must "transcend himself for a moment as he contacts the universal themes of existence. The key [being] to go beyond oneself in a single moment . . . by realizing that we are part of nature."[17] Robert Spiess similarly notes that a "haiku is not made of self-expression, but rather a full receptivity and universal acceptance."[18] Spiess then accounts for the American haiku poet's inability to develop the selfless state desired in a classic haiku poetics:

> One reason, possibly the main one, why cognitive, conceptual or intellective comprehension of a now-moment of awareness is best excluded from haiku is that it tends to establish a subject-object relation, in which the haiku poet remains outside the object. Whereas deep feeling in the haiku poet is dynamic and moves toward, or even with, the object of the awareness and unites with it. Then the poet is able to innerly experience it, in its essence and particular rhythm.[19]

Western poetics precludes the union of the subject and the object, a union flawlessly illustrated in Gurga's haiku, because the subject is underscored and the object is objectified in the Western moral-ironic tradition that conceptualizes nature through allegory. American haiku poets, as a whole, have yet to relieve themselves of this tradition and its evasions, such as the imaginative or poetic treatment of the object as only a mental image, and to master "transpersonal" phenomenologies of subjectivity and objectivity. The majority of our contemporary American poets thus tend in their haiku toward either ego-centered, consciously "poetic" exercises in the Western figurative tradition of poetry, dramatically ironic, if perhaps contrived, moments, bald, often impressionistic, nature portraits, or, to a lesser extent, experiments with surrealism, concrete poetry techniques, and the stylistically self-conscious underscoring of Zen-like experiences.

Nonetheless, during the fourth generation of American haiku one notes the growth of haiku societies, with distinct centers in Seattle, San Francisco, Gualala, Santa Fe, Dubuque, Raleigh, Rochester, New York City, Boston, Hamilton, Toronto, and Ottawa; the production of important books of haiku criticism and translation, including Betty Drevniok's *Aware* (1980), George Swede's *The Modern English Haiku* (1981), Hiroaki Sato's *One Hundred Frogs, From Renga to Haiku to English* (1983), William J. Higginson's *The Haiku Handbook* (1985), *On Love and Barley: Haiku of Bashō*, translated by Lucien Stryk (1985), *From the Country of Eight Islands, An Anthology of Japanese Poetry*, translated by Hiroaki Sato and Burton Watson (1986), and *Bashō and His Interpreters, Selected Hokku with Commentary*, translated by Makoto Ueda (1991); the compilation of haiku anthologies, such as *Erotic Haiku*, edited by Rod Willmot (1983), *HAIKU, Canadian Anthology*, edited by Dorothy Howard and André Duhaime (1985), *The Haiku Anthology, Haiku and Senryu in English*, edited by Cor van den Heuvel (1986), *Milkweed, A Gathering of Haiku*, edited by Marshall Hryciuk (1987), and *Rise and Fall of Sparrows,* edited by Alexis Rotella (1991); and the appearance of important volumes of haiku, including ones by Eric Amann, Nick Avis, Bob Boldman, L. A. Davidson, Charles Dickson, Lee Gurga, James William Hackett, Penny Harter, Elizabeth Searle Lamb, Lenard D. Moore, Alan Pizzarelli, Lee Richmond, Alexis Rotella, Robert Spiess, Ruby Spriggs, Wally Swist, Cor van den Heuvel, Anita Virgil, Nick Virgilio, Rod Willmot, John Wills, and Virginia Brady Young.

The fourth generation of American haiku poets has through experimentation all but obliterated the requisite form and substance of classic Japanese haiku: there is a consistent lack of seasonal references, surrealist techniques and figurative expression are introduced, regular prosody is eliminated, and human, rather than nature, subjects are more increasingly emphasized. Contemporary American haiku has been made a poetic vehicle for eroticism, psychological expression, and political and social commentary. The representation of the haiku image has been transformed by modernist stylistics and concrete pictorialism. Responding to these changes, Cor van den Heuvel in the "Preface" to his revised edition of *The Haiku Anthology* (1986) addresses the nature of such American haiku: "After about twenty-five years of English language haiku do we know what haiku is? There seems to be no general consensus—which may be a sign of its health and vitality."[20] Yet while coolly celebrating this rapid development of American haiku that reflects the characteristic American interest in experimentation, he seems at the end of the "Preface" to make a plea for a kind of haiku that incorporates the deep metaphysical weight envisioned for it by Bashō. And, in fact, this kind of haiku does often occur in the work of contemporary American haiku poets.

Japanese classic haiku inherits a canon of aesthetic experience associated with Japanese poetry as a whole. Experience, particularly that of nature, is thought to evoke a sympathetic emotional response from man through the mechanism of *aware* ("pathos"). The objects of experience stimulate us with a peculiar awareness of their existential solitude as distinct beings. This exchange is represented in the phrase *mono no aware* ("pathos of things"), which, according to Makoto Ueda, "refers to sadness or melancholy arising from a deep, empathic appreciation of the ephemeral beauty manifested in nature, human life, or a work of art."[21] This aesthetic value when coupled with elements from Zen Buddhism leads to the emotion of *sabi* ("patina" but, more generally, "loneliness") that is the key to Bashō's understanding of haiku. H. F. Noyes underscores the prerequisite Zen-like state of objective openness to *mono no aware* in his definition of *sabi* as "the lonely quality that each thing has in its singular existence, when observed from a state of detachment."[22] Makoto Ueda moreover stresses the cosmic dimension of this phenomenological exchange when he describes *sabi* as "spiritual serenity through immersion in the egoless impersonal life of nature—complete absorption of the petty ego into the vast, powerful, magnificent universe . . . "[23]

It is commonly thought that Bashō introduces these valuations of *sabi* with the following haiku:

kare eda ni   on a dead branch
karasu no tomari keri the crow settles—
aki no kure   autumn evening

Although Bashō uses other concepts to describe emotion, images, and technical treatment in haiku, the idea of *sabi* dominates his poetics. This haiku evokes a selfless union with the mood of *sabi* in nature, here represented through stark images of mutability—the dead branch, autumn, evening. A crow adds its potentially ominous presence to these images, but nonetheless "settles" into the scene. The poet's meditative fusion with the impermanence of nature precipitates a Zennian metaphysical awareness that likewise allows him to settle into the scene in an act of somber spiritual awakening. His consciousness nakedly confronts the essential pathos of elemental physical manifestation. This highlighting of pathos in turn all but provokes the awareness that a metaphysical permanence underlies physical change.

The phenomenological circuit of classic haiku creation and its precipitated instantaneous realization, what Bashō calls the "flash of insight," may be described as follows: 1. the poet experiences two nature images or sense perceptions, A and B; 2. the given haiku represents these images or sense perceptions, which, through their observed interrelation, evoke a realization, C; 3. the reader or listener responds to images A and B, and then to the evoked realization, C. If we recall the three main ideas of Buddhist thought: ". . . the evanescence of all things, the selflessness of all elements . . . , and the bliss of Nirvana . . . ,"[24] we may offer a complete poetics of classic haiku. The subject, or poet, has an awareness of the mutability of all nature, and therefore has a mood of *sabi* or loneliness. The contemplated object, or images A and B, stands in its ontological selflessness as the scene within this mood of loneliness. The haiku moment of the realization of the interdependent relation of mood and scene, C, evokes a "transcendent" yet aesthetically melancholy awareness of the enigmatic spiritual truth that *samsara* (physical change) equals *nirvana* (metaphysical permanence).

The long tradition of classic Japanese haiku begun with Bashō's poetics of *sabi* can be said in sum to be determined by the values of simplicity, timelessness, and silence.[25] The value of simplicity incorporates Bashō's idea that haiku subjects should be expressed in a straightforward, unadorned manner unsupported by "poetic" stylization. These subjects should also be drawn from the common things of nature, like Bashō's frog, which will reveal their pregnant essences when a poet as an egoless subject fuses himself with the emotion he finds in those essences. When Bashō says, "Learn about a pine tree from a pine tree," he means that a haiku poet should let things reveal their own emotionally resonant realities rather than impose his own emotions, conceptions, or poetic mannerisms upon these realities. The value of timelessness incorporates Bashō's view that haiku subjects provide a universal insight into life. When one looks at the things of nature in their ontologic simplicity, he experiences, in Buddhist terms, their "suchness" or "things just as they are." This state of simplicity in things is timeless because it suggests or hints at the cosmic permanence that supports its existence despite its and every material being's inevitable dissolution. Thus Bashō's decidedly temporal frog prompted the realization that *samsara* (immanence) and *nirvana* (transcendence) are interrelated. The value of silence incorporates Bashō's concept of *sabi* which he associated with quietness and receptive attention.[26] The revelation of haiku subjects in their simplicity and timelessness occurs only in silence, which is a metaphysical as well as a physical state. The splash made by Bashō's frog thus changes the nature of the silence in the pond scene and induces a profound state of consciousness that in turn prompts Bashō's insight into the cosmic nature of things.

The contemporary Canadian haiku poet Michael Dudley sums up the relevance of what resemble classic Japanese haiku modes of attention to modern English-language haiku:

> Haiku is a genre which simply refuses to play cerebral monopoly with questions of the universe's existence. Instead, haiku explores reality through an unveiling of things as they are—without the confounding worldwide pastime of distortion. This manner of approach is representative of haiku's ultimate purpose: by focusing—with sensory directness—a reader's attention upon the veritable, seemingly insignificant, and often casually overlooked incidents, relationships, and emotions of day to day

living, the haiku reveals those things that both subtly and dramatically serve as objective metaphors of our reality.[27]

That the fourth generation of American and Canadian haiku poets is exploring such modes of subjectivity and objectivity, sometimes out of an informed knowledge of Japanese haiku poetics, attests to the presiding importance of classic Japanese haiku values to the haiku form as a whole.

Perhaps the most significant element of haiku, aside from its allusive brevity, has been its identification with seasonal elements in nature. The modern world, at least in the urban centers, has made it difficult to consistently maintain this sensitivity to nature and its cycles. Yet contemporary English-language haiku poets nonetheless are determining the significance of nature and of man's relation to nature in their haiku. Paul O. Williams represents the profound literal and metaphysical separation that exists between man and nature in this haiku:

> a cat watches me
> across the still pond,
> across our difference

Marianne Bluger's haiku offer a delicate perception likewise of the encounter between man and nature, as in her haiku in which cows calmly watch a flat tire being repaired. Leatrice Lifshitz highlights such encounters with an impressionable response to evoked emotions, like the shock felt when she is suddenly confronted by the geese whose tracks she had been following. Nick Avis' haiku sensitively depict human emotion in conjunction with a natural event or object in a moment of time, such as the evoked emotion from noticing new snow while reading a letter from (presumably) his beloved. Both David Elliott and George Swede respond to various psychological dimensions of the boundaries between man and nature, Elliott through an attention to the placement and displacement of the subjective self, as in his haiku that commingles bare trees and thoughts, and Swede, through dramatic, often witty, events, such as in his haiku in which his face "surprisingly" reappears in the stream that he is dropping stones into.

A second major element of haiku is the mode of its attention toward the natural world. In haiku one must enter a realm of silence in which things, like Bashō's pine tree, reveal themselves. Bob Jones describes the psychological nature of this Zen-like attention as ". . . a more original self than that of the everyday ego: a no-self, merged with the spontaneity of nature, whose chief feature is emptiness, absence of the usual contents of consciousness."[28] This short haiku by Virginia Brady Young represents perfectly such a holding of nature subjects within the particular silence of haiku without the intervention of the subjective self:

> moonlight—
> a sand dune
> shifts

Four other haiku poets accent this kind of silence in their poems, Geraldine C. Little through emotional/perceptual spaces, as in her clay pot haiku, Lenard D. Moore through deft attention to atmosphere, as in the mist-covered gravestones in one of his haiku, Steve Sanfield, through an exploration of the deeper silence that surrounds experience, as in his loons haiku, and Ruby Spriggs, through an acute attention to the vital immanence of reality that is registered in silence, as in her heron haiku. June Moreau makes inroads to the borders of natural experience within such silence, often through unusual vantage points, as in her "hummingbird's voice" haiku. Likewise in this silence, Elizabeth St Jacques displays an acute sensitivity to perceptions of nature, especially light, as in her cave haiku. Finally, three haiku poets should be cited for the high quality of their stylistic treatment of their respective haiku moments in silence, Frank K. Robinson for the clarity of his images and the conciseness of his expression, as in his cold sparrow haiku, Anita Virgil for the finely-etched character of her haunting little dramas taken from nature and ordinary daily life, as in her box turtle haiku, and Alexis Rotella for the deftness of handling and the innovation of perspective of her astoundingly eclectic subjects, as in her snail in the lily haiku.

A third major element of haiku is its representation of the poet's fusion with his nature subjects in what Bashō terms being "one with nature." One must forgo the mind's tendency to appropriate or classify reality. One must be able to observe the things of nature objectively in order to participate in their vital realities. Doho, Bashō's disciple, interpreted his master on this point as meaning that one should "enter into the object, sharing its delicate life and its feelings."[29] Bashō's haiku is colored by a Taoist appreciation of the liveliness of the cosmic energy at play in all things and a Zen Buddhist appreciation of things "just as they are" in their existential distinctness. These values appear consistently in the work of Wally Swist, evoked through his sensitivity to rural and woodland nature, especially to sounds, as in this haiku:

> deep bend of the brook
> the kingfisher's chatter
> after its dive

Three other strong haiku poets in this mode are Charles Dickson whose nature subjects, such as his snowy egret, are acutely observed, Robert Spiess whose careful observations and vivid portrayals of the activities and processes of nature, such as his catfish on a stringer, are frequently in an elegiac mood, and John Wills whose emotionally deep encounters with the natural world, such as his duck on the winter lake, are reflective of an almost selfless union with nature and rural scenes. Michael McNierney's dancing wolf spider haiku likewise evokes this fusion. In a more self-conscious manner of union are Larry Gates' sharing the water with some frogs and Cor van den Heuvel's arm-folded observation of a crane.

Issa's haiku display the possibility for another kind of fusion with nature: one experienced as child-like wonderment and rapture. His haiku are also permeated by the Shinto belief that all things in nature possess some kind of inhabiting spirit. An Issa-like innocence before nature is found in this haiku by Raffael de Gruttola:

> in the house plants
> daddy longlegs
> has found a winter home

This same innocence and sympathy is also found in C. M. Buckaway's river rats, Brent Partridge's persistent cricket, Penny Harter's cellar rats, and Gary Gay's addressed cricket.

A fourth major element of haiku is its capacity to elicit a deep universal insight into the meaning of reality. Bashō characterized the highest valuation of this capacity in the term *sabi*, which in Japanese serves as a cognate for a desired antique look as well as the states of loneliness and desolation. Bashō incorporated these meanings in his understanding of *sabi* but furthermore identified *sabi* with silence and lonely beauty. He perceived these various characteristics of *sabi* in this haiku by his disciple Kyori:

> Hanamori ya
> shiroki kashira o
> tsukiawase
>
> blossom guards—
> their white heads
> facing each other

Every individual thing in nature, including man himself, stands in its solitariness under the sentence of its inevitable demise. Yet a beauty, even nobility, inheres in these things of nature which persevere in their own distinct natures despite the hovering silence of physical dissolution, as in the old guards of Kyori's haiku. The American haiku poet Lee Richmond provides an interpretation of this sublime melancholy inherent in reality in his definition of *sabi*, which was partly derived from R. H. Blyth, as "detachment in a cosmic sense which resides in all things."[30] This detachment, this existential aloneness, this nobility produces the pathetic beauty that is found in all things. This beauty is powerfully evoked in the following haiku by Joe Nutt:

the dugs of the old cow
shriveled—
late autumn wind

It is also explored by strong poets like Sandra Fuhringer through
her charged presentations of loneliness and silence, as in her
falling snow haiku, Alan Pizzarelli through his chilling images
of the loneliness of city life and its material objects, as in his
clinking metal washer haiku, Cor van den Heuvel through his
deft expressions of loneliness in ostensibly unassuming natural
and man-made subjects, as in his empty truck haiku, Nick Virgilio
through his deep evocations of loneliness edged with melancholy,
as in his autumn wreath haiku, and Lee Richmond through his
acute, almost subjective depictions of loneliness in the common-
place, as in his dust-coated chrysanthemum haiku.

A final element of haiku is its ability to incorporate a less
elevated and more cheerful relation to experience, particularly
commonplace human experience, than that perceived through *sabi*.
In his later life Bashō advocated this new poetics of haiku to
reflect his "acceptance of all things as they are."[31] Bashō used
the term *karumi* ("lightness") to mark his turn to this warm,
homey treatment of familiar things, like housecleaning, a leaking
roof, friendship, napping, neighbors, and ordinary natural events,
expressed in an unassuming style, what Bob Jones terms "clear-
sighted tenderness."[32] In this valuation of haiku, the day-to-day
world that is set within the greater cycle of nature becomes, in
all its so-called lowliness, a focus of aesthetic significance and
pleasure. This tender-hearted poetry of "ordinary" subjects is found
in this haiku by Carol Montgomery:

middle of the highway
with bells on
our old dog

It is also found in Hal Roth's lovely roses beside a shanty door,
Miriam Sagan's neighborhood filled with plum blossoms and

burnt toast, and Arizona Zipper's touchingly familiar cat in the sun.

Contemporary English-language haiku has, in sum, masterfully adopted the major elements of the haiku form, notwithstanding the enormity of its experimentation with that form. Although it may become harder and harder for most urban dwelling contemporary haiku poets to develop the deep relation to nature inherent in classic Japanese haiku, Bashō's "flash of insight" should be found in whatever experience comes their way. Thus, Anita Virgil notes that haiku provides "moments of special awareness that give one pause in the everyday world, make one feel the wonder of the ordinary seen anew."[33] One might, however, with trepidation, envision the failure of haiku in English as it grades finally into *senryu*, a Japanese poetic form similar in structure to haiku but emphasizing, usually in a humorous manner, human nature rather than nature itself. Yet Marshall Hryciuk, President of Haiku Canada, reminds us of the profound, presumably still available significance intended for the haiku in his definition of the haiku moment:

> By it I mean a spontaneously occurring condition or context in which the constituents, and there won't be many, are wholly themselves and "this worldly" and yet simultaneously and without cause or logic indicate or realize the infinity which ultimately is their source. Thus brevity and sparseness will dramatize this uncanny unity in duality, and moods such as serenity and compassion will enhance its accessiblity, but it is the moment itself, if it is with the writing that makes the haiku.[34]

Haiku was meant to convey the transcendental implications that may inhere in Hryciuk's "infinity." English-language haiku is heir to the Western poetic tradition of nature subjectively felt and resonant with figurative interpretation. English-language versions of haiku tend to translate this subjectivity into a moment of ironic drama. Haiku is, however, intended to represent a "higher" value of the haiku moment than this. Bashō is attributed with this description of haiku: "What is happening in this place at this moment." That the majority of the haiku in this anthology point, as intended by Bashō, to something more beyond the mere drama of a given moment or the artfully expressed enterprises of someone's imagination reflects that contemporary English-language haiku is still charged with the true spirit of haiku and is, indeed, flourishing.

NOTES

[1]This conjecture is based on interviews with a cross-section of Japanese society that were recorded in the video *Haiku: Short Poetry of Japan* (Seaton Findlay Productions, Ltd., 1980).

[2]This process resembles an occurrence in Zen Buddhism in which a sudden sound or movement, like the frog's splash in this haiku, is thought to be enough to precipitate such instantaneous spiritual enlightenment. And see the purported dialogue between Bashō and his Zen master Buccho recorded in *On Love and Barley: Haiku of Bashō*, trans. and intro. Lucien Stryk (Penguin Books, 1985), 15 for a probably apocryphal source, in a Zen Buddhist context, of the world's most familiar haiku. Likewise, such haiku resemble the Zen Buddhist *koan*, a short enigmatic verbal puzzle whose non-rational solution is thought to lead one to enlightenment. Some modern haiku poets in fact publish original *koan* with their haiku.

[3]Bob Jones, "Haiku Objectivity: The Letting-Be of What Is," *Modern Haiku* XXII: 2 (1991), 47.

[4]"Preface," *1992 Anthology of International Haiku Poets* (Haiku International Association, 1992), 5. I have tried to address this difference in my 1991 lecture, "Lost in the Translation: Subjectivity and Objectivity in Japanese and American Haiku," which was presented at the annual meeting of the American Comparative Literature Association, San Diego, CA. Some of the material in the "Introduction" to this present anthology is taken from that lecture.

[5]*New and Selected Speculations on Haiku* (Modern Haiku Press, 1988), 10.

[6]See Earl Miner, "From Renga to Haikai and Haiku" in his *Japanese Linked Poetry* (Princeton University Press, 1979) for an account of the early development of haiku.

[7]See *Modern Japanese Haiku: An Anthology*, ed. and trans. Makoto Ueda (University of Toronto Press, 1976) for a thorough discussion and representation of these transformations.

[8]See Elizabeth Searle Lamb, "Historical Notes on Haiku in English in North America" in *HAIKU, Canadian Anthology*, ed. Dorothy Howard and André Duhaime (éditions Asticou, 1985) for a detailed history of North American haiku up to the early eighties.

[9]See Ruby Spriggs' hyacinth haiku in this anthology for a response to the poetics of Williams' poem.

[10]*The Dharma Bums* (Signet, 1958), 48.

[11]"The Role of Haiku in Poetry Therapy" in his *The Modern English Haiku* (Columbine Editions, 1981), 40.

[12]*The Haiku Anthology*, ed. Cor van den Heuvel (Anchor Press/Doubleday, 1974), 256.

[13]*The Haiku Anthology* (1974), 267.

[14]*The Haiku Anthology* (1974), 271.

[15]*The Haiku Anthology* (1974), 272.

[16]*The Haiku Anthology* (1974), 268.

[17]"Therapeutic Haiku," *Dragonfly* 14:1 (1985-86), 44.

[18]"Speculations," *Modern Haiku* XVI:2 (1985), 74.

[19]"Speculations," 75.

[20]"Preface to the Second Edition," *The Haiku Anthology, Haiku and Senryu in English* (Simon & Schuster, 1986), 19.

[21]*Bashō and His Interpreters, Selected Hokku with Commentary* (Stanford University Press, 1991), 428.

[22]"Definitions: Sabi in Haiku," *Dragonfly* 15:4 (1991), 6.

[23]*Matsuo Bashō* (Kodansha International, 1982), 30.

[24]*Sources of Japanese Tradition*, Vol. 1, comp. Ryusaku Tsunoda, Wm. Theodore de Bary, and Donald Keene (Columbia University Press, 1958), 258.

[25]These three characteristics are derived from a discussion of haiku in the video *Haiku: Short Poetry of Japan.*

[26]See Ueda, *Matsuo Bashō*, 52 and Miner, *Japanese Linked Poetry*, 117 for discussions of this association.

[27]"Forward," *A Man in a Motel Room* (High/Coo Press, 1986), 5-6.

[28]"Haiku Objectivity: The Letting-Be of What Is," 44.

[29]*On Love and Barley: Haiku of Bashō*, trans. Stryk, 14.

[30]"Preface," *Fireflies* (Black Swan Books, 1989), xi.

[31]Ueda, *Matsuo Bashō*, 62.

[32]"Haiku Plainness: The Eloquence of the Ordinary," *Modern Haiku* XXIII:2 (1992), 76.

[33]"Introduction," *One Potato Two Potato Etc* (Peaks Press, 1991), xiii.

[34]"Editor's Preface," *Milkweed, A Gathering of Haiku*, ed. Marshall Hryciuk (Nietzsche's Brolly, 1987), 2.

Haiku Moment

BERNARD M. AARONSON

From every side
the skies grow black—
the gathering crows

It also rained
pink magnolia blossoms
upon the lawn

The crows unseen,
I hear them cawing, cawing
in the falling snow

SUEZAN AIKINS

Whirling snowflakes
the cries of snow buntings
somewhere above

sleeting dawn
frozen bird tracks
outside our door

whistling winds
a loon surfaces, beakfull
of waving crab legs

ANN ATWOOD

Summer is over.
A horse walks its reflection
along the lake's edge

Twilight growing
into the shape
of the mourning dove's call

Finally
    from the lily's white funnel
    day trickles out

how visible
is water charged
        with moonlight

NICK AVIS

waking from a dream . . .
only the sound of snowflakes
on the windowpane

november nightfall
the shadow of the headstone
longer than the grave

the telephone
rings only once
autumn rain

stepping from stone to stone
across the stream
the autumn moon

deep inside the faded wood a scarlet maple

midday heat
my cat on its back
y a w n s   at the sky

remembering the lie
i told her
crocus in midwinter

reading her letter
    new snow
        on the branches

we say we're sorry
    the easter lily begins
                to open

night curtain
    the autumn moonlight
    finds a small tear

WINONA BAKER

all the flowers cropped
they came so silently
the black-tailed deer

twisted arbutus
carving waves
attack the rock

moss-hung trees
a deer moves into
the hunter's silence

FRANCINE BANWARTH

a circle of light
the long necks of the swans
dipping in

in cellar darkness
where potatoes lie sprouting
falls a wedge of light

HERB BARRETT

Under autumn skies
park picnic tables
piled with leaves

November garden
a plastic sunflower
spinning   spinning

M. L. BITTLE-DeLAPA

starting to rain
shower of petals
on last year's garden

paling twilight
behind the black branch
behind the black branch

firefly there
not there
there

TOM BLESSING

the doe
carefully places her hoof
in the spring mud

MARIANNE BLUGER

rain-rinsed twilight
a motionless toad
claims the walk

flat tire
the cows just stand and slowly
turn to look

cloudy afternoon
a white chrysanthemum
just one

with what enviable impudence
the cabbage white sails
over the crowded turnstile

buzzing with flies
the heifer holds
her steady gaze

ah   these soft spring nights
full of bawling cats
and lilac!

utterly still
an old blue heron
in the sparkling shoals

twisted old lilacs
one more year
perfuming this yard

BOB BOLDMAN

locking the door
shutting my eyes
   the wind still inside my head

distant lightening
    lightening
her touch

composing me a drake in a spruce tree

whatever I wanted to say to her
   the red maple
listens

dawn
loosened
leaf by leaf

utterly still
the bluejay cries
utterly what i am

dark
moths moving
the distant mountain

JOHN BRANDI

A frog too
crosses the log bridge
from the beanfield

After the argument
—a gardenia petal
on the table.

In the rain
before the dawn: snails
migrating

The trail narrows:
deer prints
        and mist

No backward
No forward
        in the autumn rain

The rumps
of the horses —darker
after the storm

CHUCK BRICKLEY

a car
at the cliff's edge—
the Milky Way

the ledger blurs . . .
through the half-closed blinds
                    autumn moon

sheet lightning:
the face near the top
of the ferris wheel

the crow
whets its bill on the curb—
autumn wind

BEATRICE BRISSMAN

The way silence waits
and waits . . . for the next
cry of the loon

NAOMI Y. BROWN

red ants zig-zag
with a dead scorpion
afternoon heat

dusk settles—
in rattling mesquite pods
a cicada's faint voice

C. M. BUCKAWAY

July afternoon—
a couple of river rats
grooming their whiskers

Tinkling brook:
  flirting with a ripple
    a dragonfly.

The autumn moon shines
whitely on my loneliness:
lonely too the night.

Among the poplars
in a sudden stir of wind
a white owl cries out

Closing my eyelids
just before going to sleep
I hear the blizzard.

Alone at dusk . . .
many things bring remembrance . . .
summer butterfly.

MARGARET CHULA

wind blows
the last brown leaves
    clenched fingers

sudden shower
in the empty park
a swing still swinging

soft spring rain
the cat licks
the cabbage leaves

from the attic
the scutter of squirrels
    autumn rain

TOM CLAUSEN

downpour—
a duck waddles away
from the pond

daybreak frost
the sound of leaves falling
through leaves

DENISE CONEY

after the storm
I cannot find
the snowman's eyes

full moon—
a beaver slaps the pond's surface

second snowfall—
and still the leaves
            cling

yellow on yellow . . .
a swallowtail among the buttercups

STEVE DALACHINSKY

spring
without anyone knowing
tree blossoms

L. A. DAVIDSON

such a twittering
under the eaves New Year's day
the same old sparrows

on the roof
of the tenement
      sunflowers

through a closed motel window
still hearing the meadowlark

Monday morning
sunshine on a snowman
in the empty park

snow predicted;
on the coffee table
white narcissus

in a blizzard
  the city becoming
  these few blocks

What to say?
  forced forsythia
  on a winter day

on shore alone
as the ebbing tide
takes the moon with it

crossing the table
  beside a book on zen
  the cockroach pauses

RAFFAEL DE GRUTTOLA

in the house plants
daddy longlegs
has found a winter home

touched by the moon
pines
heavy with snow

endless day—
a train whistle widens
in the cold air

after some silence
a cowbell intrudes
into the cornfield

floating upriver
the garbage barge
with seagulls

CHARLES DICKSON

yellow trout lilies—
in and out of the boathouse
nesting swallows

marsh twilight
a nesting osprey
whistles softly

mountain pool
in its clarity small stones
and the flash of minnows

standing on one foot,
the goose stretches a leg—
pink sunset

                              migrating geese
         one falls farther and farther
behind

sagging footbridge—
on both sides of the brook
white laurel blossoms

field of Queen Anne's lace—
a black butterfly settles
on a stone

dense fog
a mockingbird
fills it

splash of wild plums
falling from marshside boughs
slow step of a crane

September gust—
the starflower's last white petals
snatched away

twilight storm
another stone topples
from the pasture wall

winter beach . . .
    tinkling trills
        of water pipits

abandoned pasture
in fallen snarls of barbed wire
white of meadowsweet

out of the fog bank
              croak
of a snowy egret

MIKE DILLON

October hot spell—
the hedge never so alive
with hornets

Parked bulldozer
half-done with the house:
spring moon

Winter rain:
a crow peers down
from the power line

PATRICIA DONEGAN

I lay down
all the heavy packages—
autumn moon.

Last night lightning
this morning
the white iris.

People are gone
& the beach is empty—
the green reeds.

Tonight
the cypress tree & I
lean into the wind.

BETTY DREVNIOK

Lilac scent:
coming upon the remains
of the old chimney

Someone calls; someone answers.
Evening river-fog
hides the far shore

Spring snow
on the beach
a small green pail   turned over

Full moon at midnight:
holding between both hands
the white peony blossom

Morning coffee:
everywhere I gaze
pine boughs weighed down with new snow

MICHAEL DUDLEY

lulling me to sleep
the rain
then waking me

oaring not moving the lilies

VIRGINIA EGERMEIER

Same old road—but
over the fog, a giant oak
I never saw before

Spring thaw:
the old pine leans a little
farther this year

BERNARD LIONEL EINBOND

frog pond . . .
a leaf falls in
without a sound

the thousand colors
in her plain brown hair—
morning sunshine

LESLEY EINER

before the quail
its querying call . . .
again

holding
the shape of the wind
the frozen pines

DAVID ELLIOTT

A blue heron
flying south
over the long straight road

Dark so soon . . .
   down the creek in ripples
     a full moon

A spider climbs
the white curtain
   snow still falling

Below zero
but this week the sun shines
right on the kitchen table

The silence after geese
    fade from sight
part of me following

Hard to be some-
  one in all
    this snow falling

Some year
they won't find me here . . .
  returning geese

Spring thaw—
even this tiny stream
making such a roar

4 a.m.
only two peepers
still at it

Such lightness
        apple boughs
        in the breeze

October sunset
all the way to the horizon
a flock of starlings

51

Among leafless trees
  too many thoughts
  in my head

MARGARITA MONDRUS ENGLE

drifting fog
   two crows on a wire
   touching beaks

rush hour
   far above the line of headlights
   a full moon

old orchard
   a spider climbs onto
   the setting sun

afternoon sun
  only the neighborhood hawk
  has someplace to go

dusk
  the great blue heron
  folding its neck

autumn night
  nose to the window
  a ghost-white cat

RUTH ESHBAUGH

cold moon
alone
in the whippoorwill's cry

SISTER MARY THOMAS EULBERG

only that star
    and I
            alone

through window frames
of the unfinished building
December sunset

no need
for the night light
the glow of maples

everything's strange
in this boarding house
only the moon is real

fresh snow
   all names obliterated
   on the headstones

DEE EVETTS

Within the sunken punt stillwater

willows turn silver
a long moment before
the wind

the river
going over
the afternoon
going on

LIZ FENN

First day of spring
The goldfish
Circles his bowl

ROSS FIGGINS

autumn shadows—
the scarecrow bends forward
closer to the earth

twilit pasture—
voices of frogs fill
the forgotten bucket

SARAH FITZJARRALD

so still . . .
 only the falling plum blossoms

ELLEN FLORMAN

Midwinter night—
a dead spider
still clinging to its web

A cold moon—
black cat's shadow
slips in with the rain

SYLVIA FORGES-RYAN

sparrow chirping—
on this winter morning
its white breath

January coldness—
snowman's shadow reaching
our windowpane

snowdrifts getting deeper:
what do they mean—
my dreams . . .

MARIE FORSYTH

quiet pond . . .
the red carp swims
through a white cloud

MARCO FRATICELLI

Outside the cemetery
A leaning telephone pole
Tied to a tree

The old man
Sweeping leaves from the lawn
First snowfall

Morning train—
Entering the dark tunnel
Suddenly: my face

SANDRA FUHRINGER

the open grave . . .
a leaf falls
in the moonlight

Autumn wind
opening . . . and closing
a screen door

Moonless night—
the old dog
barks at a scarecrow

one autumn cricket
fills the garden with shadows

Straight down
  snow falls and falls . . .
   the silence deepens

rain all day the cat's yawn

alone on the lake
until the loon's cry
. . . still alone

FREDERICK GASSER

Yard sale:
balanced on a china cup
a swallowtail

late evening—
the dog's hair smells
of peonies

abandoned sidewalk—
the thickness of wild grasses
between the cracks

BOB GATES

winter burial
on the bare branch
a cocoon

LARRY GATES

a cloud on the water
I float, half-submerged
with the frogs

a quiet afternoon;
the old turtle drying out
beside the still water

GARRY GAY

September stillness;
    the long wait for the heron
       to move

Early morning frost;
mine are the only footprints
to the dead sparrow

Seal voices
carry from the rocks . . .
the fog

3:15 am
    still I can't fall asleep;
      you too cricket?

Hiking
into the clouds
the view within

Her mailbox
leans into the honeysuckle
rusted and empty

The yellow lily;
  in the water
    in the rain

Late summer moon—
the cricket remains silent
in the glass jar

ROBERT GIBSON

Beyond the lawn
Where uncared-for grasses grow
Wild daisies—

The autumn moon
Rising later and rounder
Tonight

Sunrise
Thirty pound salmon roll
In Babine river

BARRY GOODMANN

                teasing the crab
            the ebb
                    the flow

LeROY GORMAN

nitefall
my wife & I embrace
a shadow

first snow
lites our bedroom
she puts on the flowered sheets

rainpuddles on the garden
I pass
my image

a brown leaf floats
where yesterday I swam
with a friend

in the hills above us
silver snow
is filling the darkness

cool wind off the river
I ask my wife
the time

LARRY GROSS

cicadas stop
but not
my ears

dangling
from the impatiens bloom
caterpillar

the still air
before and after
my passing

by firelight
listening to the silence
of things we can't see

LEE GURGA

first spring day—
beyond the woodpecker
beyond the moon

hillside of troutlily—
in a mossy log's shadow
the single bloom

trying the old pump a mouse pours out

each waiting
for the other's silence—
April birdsong

spot of sunlight—
on a blade of grass the dragonfly
changes its grip

going out of my way
to crunch them as I walk;
first leaves of autumn

ROSAMOND HAAS

from pondview bridge
how white the mallards' tails
upended in the breeze!

LORRAINE ELLIS HARR

The time it takes—
for snowflakes to whiten
the distant pines

PENNY HARTER

all night
the sound of your breathing
the autumn wind

receding train—
smoke drifts
into the autumn trees

autumn twilight—
  only the foam
    of the waterfall

January morning—
among the cornstalks the necks
of Canada geese

even the cellar rats
sleeping late
this snowy morning

fallen thistle . . .
still the down floats
over the neighbor's hedge

DORIS HEITMEYER

November
   no sound from the mourning dove
     except its wings

Between lace curtains
   the white cat's eyes
     follow a snowflake

Wind chill minus five
   the piercing whistles
     of the starlings

The cardinal
    wipes his beak on a twig and
        takes another berry

Through the hum
    of the window fan—
        cicada?

Inside the bottle
    the firefly's light
        even brighter

CHRISTOPHER HEROLD

sunrise
    blooms in the purple
        of a wild iris

unlatched gate—
to and fro a lizard rides
the creaking breeze

deserted beach—
the hollow sound of waves
collapsing

from a tiny hole
nautilus chambers spiral:
growing emptiness

Steller's jay—
in one eye twinkles
the eclipsing sun

HARVEY HESS

narcissus flowers . . .
their shadows on the wall
belong to themselves

WILLIAM J. HIGGINSON

the tick, tick
of snow on the reeds . . .
sparrow tracks

wet snow—
another color or two
on the sycamore boughs

Holding the water,
  held by it—
    the dark mud.

Without a thought,
  the neighbor's backyard
  turns green.

The clock
  chimes chimes and stops,
  but the river . . .

ANNA HOLLEY

one eye open
the cat eyes the fly,
the long slow day

In the poppy field
a black butterfly separates
from its shadow

white heron
all but its cry
lost in haze

looking back
at the fullest moon
a round-faced frog

a crow flies
becoming the darkness
on an autumn evening

chestnuts patter down,
in fits and starts
cold cicadas cry

light from a doorway
crosses the empty road;
autumn dusk

MAGNUS HOMESTEAD

Deep stillness—
Out of morning light
A lotus unfolds

Railroad track
Thick with rust
A sunflower ripens

GARY HOTHAM

this day in history—
the air
the leaves fall through

the sound they make
the sound I make
autumn leaves

rest stop—
in the darkness
the grass stiff with frost

our yard
our neighbor's yard
leaves piled on leaves

no one moves—
the winter evening
darkens the room

DOROTHY HOWARD

tall pines—
the setting sun too
lingers

lunar eclipse
our eyes looking
in the same direction

MARSHALL HRYCIUK

over a field of stones
            in the mist

   a wireless telephone pole

       gnarled cherrytrees
a crow on the bridge
          doesn't budge

through the screen, through the rain
an island
in mist

KEN HURM

winter moon
taking all night to cross
so small a pond

VIRGIL HUTTON

Cloudless spring sky;
off and on all day
the caw of a crow

Spring dawn;
young tree just big enough
to rest a blackbird

Migrating swallows;
  the gentle fall
    of rain and leaves

Autumn wind
louder and louder—
the rattle of leaves

FOSTER JEWELL

Still there
in the shrinking puddle
my reflection.

Not hearing the silence—
until
the whip-poor-will!

Last raindrop
nears end of twig . . .
nearing it . . . nearing it . . .

RANDY JOHNSON

slower than the rest
now and then
a big flake falls

melting into the night
the red October dusk
the maple leaves

ROBERT N. JOHNSON

the dark hawk
perched there, hangs his wings
  first rain

winter cottonwoods
the sky between them
windblown, blue

JEAN JORGENSEN

afternoon hush
click of the dragonfly's wings
through tall grass

JIM KACIAN

the door slams shut—
no one around
but the south wind

heat lightning—
fireflies cross the meadow
without a sound

plum blossoms
falling
in the wind, in the calm

summer wind—
the sheen of the tall grass
when it bends

LEROY KANTERMAN

Sunset . . .
The scarecrow stretches
Across the field

ADELE KENNY

moonrise:
at the edge of the woods
we listen

winter solstice—
sun
in the crow's eye

on the wet street
the moon moves in and out
of itself

sleepless night—
in every room
the sound of the wind

MICHAEL KETCHEK

ten minutes to five
the goldfish
swim back and forth

light morning mist
only the roller coaster
rises above the trees

waves crash
against the pier—the bottle
slips from my hand

JERRY KILBRIDE

christmas night
the silence behind
the wind

northern lights:
my breath
on the window

mother lode country,
each morning my eyes search
the same mountain

GEORGE KLACSANZKY

early morning
fishing boat full of
pelicans

orange carp
lost in the reflection
red maple leaves

with each receding
wave—the sound of
pebbles

ELSIE KOLASHINSKI

already the bees
have discovered the flowers
on the new grave

dry creek bed
old cottonwood
leans on its shadow

ELIZABETH SEARLE LAMB

a white horse
drinks from the acequia
  blossoming locust

the old irrigation ditch   gathering in   autumn dusthaze

for this one moment
curve of the horned owl's flight
above the frozen meadow

the elk herd
moving down the ridge
—an early snow

early blizzard
the faintest cries of wild geese
in the dark, in the snow

in morning sun two white horses   the autumn aspen

field of wild iris—
the pinto pony
kicks up his heels

before firstlight
the wild plum blossoms
whiten the dry ditch

in the last light
a hummingbird moth visits
the white petunia

and after . . .
drifting toward sleep,
spring peepers

JANE K. LAMBERT

Summer shower:
still the mockingbird splashes
in the birdbath

DAVID E. LeCOUNT

last night's rain—
a curl in the leaf where
a caterpillar sleeps

turtle skeleton—
ants going in one leg
and out the other

dusk dimming—
a bat drinks from the pool
without a pause of wing

KENNETH C. LEIBMAN

November morning—
the heron's legs
lost in steam

no breeze—
the branch
where a bird was

cow pasture—
beyond NO TRESPASSING
    egrets

sunflowers:
one facing
    the other way

MINNA LERMAN

the way the breeze
ruffles his fur
dead cat

even in the owl's swoop   no sound

barren maple
in a spider's web
a dry leaf

box turtle
all night   staring
at the ceiling

coming in on the tide   the moon

raining again
          peony stems
                    are long

LEATRICE LIFSHITZ

my tracks . . . their tracks . . .
suddenly face to face
with returning geese

snowstorm—
the old snowman leaning
into it

winter thaw—
the deer's blood still frozen
to its face

without a breeze
the silence of the windchime
by the stream

glass doors—
the old cat pauses before
entering the night

nameless
again the windowsill plant
insists on blooming

REBECCA LILLY

Spring clouds—
the thoroughbreds
nod through their breath.

Where I spotted the deer
the deep-worn path
disappears into grass

Evening rain—
the downrush of day
into shadow

GERALDINE C. LITTLE

frosted sedge grass—
the crane on one leg holds
the silence

coming home
    in the empty bed
    just winter moon

how delicately
a black cat crosses
the frozen field

winter solstice:
    a snow goose lifts from its shadow
    towards the light

Full winter moon:
the icicle
the icicle's shadow

on the bank
a single light
moves through the trees

the bright silence of sun in a clay pot

Listening
  as the wave retreats
          into itself

in the polished doorknob
    we daily touch
        passage of geese

summer afternoon
    a beach umbrella
    no one comes to

Eaves
    pulling sound
        from the wind

MATTHEW LOUVIÈRE

Moonlit night
—the scarecrow's hat
bright with rime

These chrysanthemums
appear so gaunt today—
November wind

The white cat
lowers its whiskers—
first snow

Winter wind—
whistling through the holes
of the mailbox

The goose—
stretching its shadow
stretching its neck

Winter fog—
crow pacing
the bare branch

Dark shadow
of the white chrysanthemum
—the quiet room

A mule
rolling in the dust—
the shadowy moon

Twilight
seeping into
the stone

White butterfly—
so still
on the black branch

Thunder
—the mirror shifts
in its frame

Spring wind—
sweeping the clouds
from puddle to puddle

Heavy summer air
—the black cat walks around
in circles

One dragonfly
—the whole rice field
astir

PEGGY LYLES

nip of fall . . .
a rabbit's toothmarks
in magnolia leaves

first frost . . .
on a silver card tray
wild persimmons

Tea fragrance
from an empty cup . . .
the thin winter moon

TOM LYNCH

almost asleep
a breeze wakes me—
northern lights

suddenly here
grasshopper on my knee
suddenly gone

BARBARA McCOY

A few red tomatoes
among the hard, green ones—
falling leaves

Autumn sunset—
Blue shadows on the mountain
meet blue shadows in the lake

January cold
On the fencepost an old green rug
littered with straw

Snow beyond the pane;
In a crystal bud vase
the white rose unfolds . . .

anne mckay

in the april orchard
that thin black bird
                    . . . waiting

from her window
at sundown
at moondown

DOROTHY McLAUGHLIN

alone in the rain—
even my shadow
washed away

drifts of snow—
spider webs whitening
corners of the shed

apple orchard
    empty twisted branches
        glisten in the rain

no stars tonight
but the fireflies so close
you can touch them

DONALD McLEOD

barnacles
still clinging
to a dead whale's belly

momentary dolphins—
woven in the curl
of a summer wave

MICHAEL McNIERNEY

the boat's horn echoes
against the far buildings—
evening lightning

wolf spider dancing
sideways on the wall

dusk

CAROL MONTGOMERY

middle of the highway
with bells on
our old dog

autumn storm
my dead aunt's
alarm ringing

in my silver
wedding shoes
. . spider webs

between pinches of goldfish food

    .   .   .   .   .

        .   .

stillness settles

LENARD D. MOORE

twilight mist;
the sparrow on the barbed wire
shifts his head

winter river:
two ducks
still in the moonlight

a moth rises
in the smoke wind . . .
the silence

plum-scented farm—
the stilled shadow
of a fox

in the moonlit breeze
    slowly falling one by one:
        white dogwood petals

moon dusk: another grasshopper hops on the wind

abandoned mill:
still the smell of pine
this summer evening

evening mist
settles on the gravestones
distant crows

hill after hill
   so many tomatoes ripening
in the hot sun

Long after sundown
the sound of ripe plums
plumping the ground

JUNE MOREAU

it's a wonder
the wind doesn't take it
the cat's shadow . . .

the sky's
whole silence
in the owl's wings

Clumps of cranberry
glisten in the snow
the sound of wild geese

sunrise . . .
the fox's tail
weighted with dew

squinting my eyes
to hear it
the hummingbird's voice

shaping itself on the pond   the spring wind

a hornet
dangles in the air
how hot it is!

MARLENE MOUNTAIN

thrush song a few days before the thrush

beyond the sink of undone dishes bird feeder

a hot day an inchworm drops from the high leaves

autumn dusk the crooked road home

cloudy day half a load of clothes in the wash

faded flowers of the bed sheets autumn night

CHARLES D. NETHAWAY, JR.

waterfall at night—
her long
              black
                        hair

spring the one dead tree

monarch—
half-flying
half-blown

late summer
just waiting for the leaves
to come on down

PATRICIA NEUBAUER

down this old lane
no one travels now
except the swallows

hesitating . . .
ahead, tree shadows cross
the moon-bright road

dusk—one by one
barn cats disappear into
the ripening wheat

black ant—in and out
over and under
white peony petals

PATRICIA NIEHOFF

as I approach them—
the trees moving
against the mountain

reaching into the mailbox
a handful of cobwebs

JOE NUTT

new leaves
a day at a time
creeping up the mountain

the squirrel's tail
curls over his head—
spring rain

silence
fills the summer meadow
circled by the hawk

sunrise
out of the black earth
a perfect radish

in the yellow sun
on the meadow—suddenly
grasshopper

tent caterpillars
munching cherry leaves—
ragged clouds

after the bellow
of a distant bull—
the gurgling creek

early frost—
on the thickened marsh
geese come together

another parting . . .
   through the dark sky
      fading sounds of geese

the dugs of the old cow
shriveled—
late autumn wind

Flickering
   in the woodpile
      the groundhog's eyes

BRENT PARTRIDGE

cooper's hawk
hunched atop a rockpile
          fog's thickening

hard rain—
the carp all gathered
under the bridge

autumn wind
a frog's singing
under my hot-tub

preceding me
all down the long beach
    flock of small birds

autumn fog
        the redwood silence
        i stop in my tracks

i carry a cricket
        back outside—
it wants in again

no two falling
the same way
cherry petals

the rest of the valleys
    and hills grow quieter—
noisy geese!

checking the breeze
        a frog's nose
                just sticks out

down into
where all the stems join
a little frog

BILL PAULY

tonight your face
in the river, father,
wrinkles with wind

seventh day of rain . . .
trying to remember
the names of things

white undersides
of birch leaves in the storm . . .
undressing each other

BRETT PERUZZI

Reflected in the river
the stillness
of early morning

dilapidated cottage
the flower box's weeds
in full bloom

ALAN PIZZARELLI

cold wind
at the knotted end of the flagpole rope
a washer . clinks

the ferris wheel turning
into the fog

in the stream
a shopping cart
fills with leaves

bitter cold
the car's horn blows
by itself

twilight
staples rust
in the telephone pole

the windowpane reflects
a tv cartoon
snow falling

the shade springs open
frozen socks on the line

in front of the go-go bar
a broken umbrella
    shakes with the wind

on the merry-go-round
that empty blue bench

nightfall
horse chestnuts hit the parked car

light rain
on the young tree
a strip of burlap   flaps

FRANCINE PORAD

crab
washed ashore
each feeler intact

drone
deep in sweet alyssum—
Indian summer

night clouds
touching
the city's aura

side by side—
　　　shrivelling camellias
　　　snowy white plum

twilight deepens
the wordless things
I know

CLAIRE PRATT

clean summer breeze
  the curtain as far out the window
    as it will go

O forsythia
  even the traffic is hushed
    in the morning sun

starless night   moving outward   the undertow

October mist
  hanging in space
   lighted globes

darkened beach   rocking on its back   winter moon

DAVID PRIEBE

Autumn cloud shadows
slowly down one mountain side
                    and up another

On a steppingstone
    in the light from the back porch
        a snail trail glistens

In shallow water
    half of the minnows
        are only shadows

GLORIA H. PROCSAL

from winter sky
  to brook
    the icy moon

out of rainy hills
they come: thin-shelled snails
and plump red worms

april sunrise
a mockingbird shakes off rain,
struggles into song

VIOLA PROVENZANO

river fog:
the legs of cranes
in field stubble

empty moonlit beach—
a little ghost crab sits
alone with the sea

cedar grove silence;
the rain's
cold drops

ANTHONY J. PUPELLO

winter chill—
suddenly, my lone reflection
in the mirror

shadows on the wall
—the cicada's call
lingers

FREDERICK A. RABORG, JR.

in the frigid wind
a single longhorn steer—
emptiness is white

ZHANNA P. RADER

Frozen moon . . .
lower and lower—
the pine's iced branches

Blue mud dauber,
shiny
even in death

Stepping
out of the mist—
pine trees

All at once:
sumac's red leaves
cricket in the house

GEORGE RALPH

from the shadows
a butterfly
     its shadow

a patch of sunlight
on the rhododendron
where the butterfly was

chilly night:
only two cicadas
back and forth

midday blizzard:
not seeing beyond the pines
not seeing the pines

ice-encrusted
in the tree's bark
old cicada shell

JANE REICHHOLD

in the dark
a young cat
full of kittens

a barking dog
little bits of night
breaking off

evening fog
a door slams
softly

        such a storm!
    falling on the roof
        all the stars

autumn wind
the way things turn around
at dusk

how snugly
this new ice fits
the old pond

October sun
deep in the doorway
deep in pumpkins

winter
hours frozen
   into snowflakes

New Year's Day
a throbbing in the swan's neck
looking north

sea lions bark
their breath comes ashore
as mist

WERNER REICHHOLD

tidepool
refilling time
   with water

fiddler crab
all of its gestures
in tune

        desert
quietly composing
        silence

BARBARA RESSLER

Easter lily
holds
the morning

DAVID RICE

surfbirds on the rock
reappearing
reappearing

LEE RICHMOND

Along this road
nobody goes,
only one fatted swan

Scolding myself,
the iris by the doorstep
somebody's trampled

In mother's voice
all of autumn's cicadas
heard it

A speckled hen
walking in dark March mud,
and I become sad

Before today
where did he come from
scarecrow

Winter chrysanthemums
friends invite me out
but these winter chrysanthemums.

The loneliness
frost growing to my nightshirt
this morning also.

Without a place to die,
crouches where he pleases:
winter fly

A winter chrysanthemum
although I close my eyes
flecked with dust

ANDY ROBERTS

salamander
        from stone to stone
in the numbing water

FRANK K. ROBINSON

drifting clouds—
a pear petal is drawn
to its reflection

through the dark
it comes to us / the slow rhythm
of the first frogs

mountain stillness . . .
trumpet vine
bright on the old barn

indian summer
in the grinding stone
a red leaf

sleepless night
on the screen a firefly
flashes

flashes

flashes

        a gentle tugging
on my line
        the late summer moon

across the road
from the sunflower patch
a sunflower

autumn moon
out of the dark hills
a flight of cranes

        so many years . . .
that inchworm
        across his stone

190

first flakes
a sparrow settles deeper
into its feathers

chrysanthemums
on the bedside table
early dusk

still white world . . .
trying to follow my ears
to the snowy owl

fog lifting
mountains
above mountains

a sparrow searches
the windowbox . . .
half-remembered faces

EMILY ROMANO

scrawny rabbit
sprawled on its side—
this heat!

through thinning mist
the bawl of the calf
                    the calf

chilly morning
possum's bare tail protrudes
from the compost pile

Indian summer
how careless the crows
among corn stubbles

quiet waters;
the slow, skating walk
of a great blue heron

dusk;
a bee burrows deeper
into the marigold

RONAN

sea gulls placing
and replacing themselves
on black rocks

MILDRED A. ROSE

Sun moves relentlessly
over the headstone
wilting flowers

Sparrows twittering
in the dim barn dust layers
the unused harness

RAYMOND ROSELIEP

piano practice
through an open window
the lilac

seance
a white
moth

footbridge
only the moon
crossing

BRUCE ROSS

abandoned house—
the lilacs just as bright
this spring

luminous moonlight—
the slow undulating of
a scavenging skunk

still spring night—
fallen dogwood petals
under the bright moon

a spider huddled
in the ceiling corner.
endless spring rain

spring chill—
on short legs the sparrow
sips from Lake Ontario

faint spring mist—
only the bright orange
of poppy blossoms

morning silence—
dull spring sunlight
on the potted cactus

loon's cry
at Burnt Rock Lake—
slow autumn clouds

early autumn sun—
a spider races across
the weathered log

the gray squirrel pair
gingerly kiss on the roof.
cloudless autumn day

autumn drizzle—
the slow ticking
of the clock

migrating monarchs
cluster along the shoreline.
thousands of wet stones

a milk-white spider
explores the morning teapot.
light autumn breezes

early morning woods—
the young deer just
stares and stares

puzzled crow's
snow covered
beak

frozen Quaker Pond—
even between the dry hummocks
deep silence

under the mallard's
careful step
breaking ice

a leaping squirrel
kicks up
sparkling snow

ALEXIS ROTELLA

At the top
of the ferris wheel,
lilac scent

soaking up the moon   the snail

The silence
of paper lanterns:
morning rain

swans   stir of his breath against my hair

Among morning-glories
the drip drip
of lingerie

An old woman with bread
waves the geese down
from the sky.

Lightning:
in the crack of a boulder,
violets.

Picking the daisy—
my mind
on the next one.

Up through the moon
the watersnake lifts
its shiny head.

I let it pass
right through me—
cicada sound.

bulging
with moonlight
the day-lily bud

Wild phlox—
another high-school friend
is gone.

A wet spot
  on the rock
    where the frog sat.

One little woodpecker
rattling
the house.

a swallowtail
        settles
on the prize-winning quilt

Does that one star
  see me
    too?

Not speaking
our shadows
keep touching

dusk:
the snail deeper
into the lily

After the first snow
rabbit tracks
connecting graves.

The gull
giving loneliness
sound

I forgot why I was angry:
deer tracks
filling with snow

winter chill
the moon moves away
from the geese

Autumn stillness—
a hornet's nest hangs over
the lake

Still on its vine
the pumpkin
in the compost.

autumn sky
the wind folds and unfolds
a flock of sparrows

HAL ROTH

sparrow
on the mailbox
empty

lifting the hay bale
crows
in morning mist

only a shanty
but these roses here
beside the door . . .

night
bending
with the river

LAWRENCE RUNGREN

kept awake all night
by the blossoming
apple tree

the cat hisses
as I touch her
cold spring rain

autumn comes
rust deepens
on the unused tracks

November dusk
an empty place where
chrysanthemums bloomed

REBECCA RUST

Overnight snow,
opening the blinds
to see the emptiness

in moonlit sea
the pier's broken pile
rising   falling

dark rainy street,
the ice cream truck bells
ringing for no one

night swamp,
one by one the crocodiles
slip into the moon

MIRIAM SAGAN

The whole neighborhood—
Plum blossoms,
Burnt toast.

Wanted to buy
white summer blouse—
Mountain still capped with snow.

Unseen at first—
The flat graves
Covered by brown oak leaves

LEWIS SANDERS

Without frog sounds—
this August night
passes into dawn

Winter rain—
my father's grave
  so many miles away

Snow predicted—
. . . slow rain
    making puddles in the dark

STEVE SANFIELD

So silent
you can almost hear
the sun.

Summer mountains:
here
all the time.

Without a moon
the sea
becomes deeper.

The loudest sound:
the quail
at dawn.

No fire.
The cat still settles
behind the stove.

The naked trees
make it colder
—this autumn moon.

Loons cry—
the deeper silence
behind.

MARGARET SAUNDERS

Through
        the autumn mist
a panting jogger

Winter stillness
the sound
of a branch breaking

GRANT SAVAGE

October evening
The only sunset
Autumn leaves

Look!!
Still a bit of snow
Snowdrops in bloom

Softly
A chickadee
Between the wind

After the storm
My friend's cat
Fishes for the moon

SHARON LEE SHAFII

Cold wind . . .
just-swept leaves
gusting back

outdoor cafe
only a cricket chirping
this fall day

Frozen dawn . . .
a metal hook banging
the flagpole

Pileated woodpecker
keeps the tree trunk
between us

after the storm
tossing starfish back
into the sea

EILEEN SHERRY

snow dusted branches
sparrow footprints
lead into the air

HELEN J. SHERRY

caught between
 old shutter slats
the harvest moon

cold wind
doves shuffle their feathers
 in unison

daybreak . . .
 snow lightens the field
 flake by flake

ebb tide . . .
 the heron's reflection
 becomes its shadow

ROB SIMBECK

full moon . . .
     the cat trotting
       up the fire escape

STEPHEN SMALL

I did nothing
about a branch that fell
on the wild azalea

DOROTHY CAMERON SMITH

even the clouds
are in a hurry
this morning

November fog
my old aunt
asks who I am

MARGARET R. SMITH

as if they owned
the late afternoon sky
swallows

trapped in the trashcan
through bared teeth, the hisses
of a young possum

TOM SMITH

new year's sun
finds one sparrow
on the white pine bough

hummingbird
in the flowering crab
cold sunlight

rainfall
the broken
iris

KAREN SOHNE

not knowing what to answer
watching the forsythia blossoms fall

looking straight into the sun
dandelions

                                      dragonfly
above its nearly still reflection
                                        dragonfly

such red tulips
not minding the rain at all

no moon tonight
our eyes are drawn
to the white chrysanthemum

rain
ticking on the leaves
the long night

walking in winter
every branching twig
against the snowfall

KEITH SOUTHWARD

Bulrushes explode
We hold each other closer
Indian summer

In the fading light
A crimson leaf sinking
To the bottom of the pool

ROBERT SPIESS

A spring breeze rises—
　　breast feathers ruffle
　　　　on the dead sparrow

Asparagus bed
　　silent in the morning mist
　　　　the wild turkeys

Evening clouds—
　　a catbird murmurs
　　　　among the lilac leaves

A dirt road . . .
　　acres of potato plants
　　　　white-flowered under the moon

Becoming dusk,—
  the catfish on the stringer
  swims up and down

a round melon
in a field of round melons
—resting dragonfly

an unspoken love—
i envy the oriole
that sings   that sings

First light:
an oval drop of water
on the mallard's back

A breeze on the stream—
with much commotion
carp are spawning by the reeds

canoeing the bend—
a hundred vocal swallows
fly from the cliff

Summer is turning—
  at the roots of the grass
  crickets rasp their song

the field's evening fog—
  quietly the hound comes
  to fetch me home

Winter wind—
  bit by bit the swallow's nest
  crumbles in the barn

RUBY SPRIGGS

within closing petals silence

rain in the night—
    in the cricket's chirp
    in the loon's call

a leaf lifts a cat stretches

nothing
  depends on
    this hyacinth blooming

even for the scarecrow a shadow

lingering on this earth   dried onions

the day dwindles into a loon's call

still hazy morning
  a bird sings a leaf falls
  a bird sings a leaf falls

to no special place
  the wind blows the leaves

on one leg
     the heron spreads its silence
     over the still lake

ELIZABETH ST JACQUES

dodging
spears of moonlight
the silver fox

mallard feather
still finding light
on his bedroom wall

march winds . . .
the mailbox
also moans

lightning flash . . .
the high shrill cry
of the midnight bat

the cave's mouth
    pulling
        in the light

swaying
    to its own music
        the wildflower

in the night barn
nothing
but cat's eyes

on a step
up to the falls
the quiet butterfly

EBBA STORY

first light . . .
a fox track deepens
with shadow

gleaming gold:
amid a russet willow
the night heron's eye

RICHARD STRAW

black horse
noses frosted grass stems—
year's end

DENVER STULL

winter ice storm;
the old cat wants out
wants in

CHRISTOPHER SUAREZ

old warehouse—
a sparrow flying
from its broken window

DAVE SUTTER

Summer storm—
the spider's web
still there.

Among the reeds
their legs disappear—
white egrets

Summer mountain:
morning mist
the only sound

GEORGE SWEDE

Falling pine needles   the tick of the clock

Into the mailbox
go all the letters
scattered clouds

Dropping stone after stone
into the lake—I keep
reappearing

After the rain
a white butterfly
on the clothesline

dusk
a lone car going the same way
as the river

Divorce proceedings over
wet leaves stick
to my shoes

Lilac-scented breeze
a floorboard creaks from
the old spinster's room

Circling higher and higher
at last the hawk pulls its shadow
from the world

Dawn   only the mountain sees me leave

Lightning flash
crows sitting under
the scarecrow

Night begins to gather   between her breasts

Broken mirror in the stream
I look more deeply
into myself

WALLY SWIST

walking farther into it
the farther it moves away
spring mist

we wake at dawn
crow calling crow
through the fog

opened so boldly
in spring snow
the red tulip

spring rain
all night
the same peeper

in the one unbroken pane
    remaining in the shed
full moon

stopping in my steps . . .
a bird who seems to know me
calling from the pines

opening into forest
    on rusted hinges
the old pasture gate

Indian summer
    cows reclining
among fallen leaves

deep bend of the brook
    the kingfisher's chatter
after its dive

sun burns off morning mist
    the far field
of pumpkins

beside the brook's rush
    New England aster
coated with frost

startled from the thicket—
the drumming pheasant's wings
fade into silence

at the edge
of the iced-over pond—
a burst of cattails

lingering
in the oak
autumn twilight

foggy morning—
the emptiness echoes
with geese

standing out
in the autumn garden
the white rose

pausing to listen . . .
the brook's icy ledges
cracking again

new moon
tightening the darkness
a cricket's ratchet

the insistent voice
of a black-capped chickadee
snowy morning

new snow:
the cottontail
licks its paws

plummeting
into a silent pool
the frozen waterfall

KENNETH TANEMURA

a single rose
blooming in the sunlight
and in my eyes

the lightning flashes
a silkworm slips
out of its cocoon

only the stone-smell
tells of it . . .
summer rain

A starry night—
the sunflowers hanging
over the riverbank

a corner
of the untended garden
white chrysanthemums

sleepless . . .
the cat purring
echoes my thoughts

K. G. TEAL

old weatherbeaten
motel sign—
full of sparrows

hush before the storm—
only this cricket
chirping

RICHARD THOMPSON

Suspended
on white rhododendron:
sunset

Surrounding the stone   silence

RICHARD TICE

A day at the office:
nothing to remind me
it's snowing

bare trees
along the avenue all the way
to the mountain

TOM TICO

Sandpipers
running along the glassy beach
on top of themselves

a windless morning
and still the plum blossoms
flutter to the ground

Beneath darkening skies
the flowers of the plum tree
whiter and whiter

Dusk . . .
the whole forest dark
except for the lilies

Engulfing
    the purple rhododendrons
    shadows of evening

a morning of fog:
    again and again the caw
    of an unseen crow

On every step
    of the old stone stairway—
    autumn leaves

SUE STAPLETON TKACH

Flooded by spring rain
path through the arboretum
finding its own way

Sooner or later
the petals fall among us
holding them gently

vincent tripi

Letting
     the cat in
     the fog in

Persimmons grow
their shadows
with them

Colouring itself across the pond the autumn wind . . .

Almost full moon . . .
a rustle of leaves
through the canyon

Abandoned ferris wheel
    encircling
        the silence

Another song—
the bird that follows me
to pond ice

Without a trail . . .
the silence of snow falling
around the mountain

ANNA VAKAR

still climbing,
a squash vine in full blossom
this cold day

in the large shadow
a white horse
with no shadow

sunlight on the snow
the brown leaves
have not let go

COR VAN DEN HEUVEL

arms folded
i watch the crane
standing on one leg

three clothespins
hold themselves on the line
March wind

under the pier
at low tide—
the evening sunlight

by the lawn's edge,
the dog barks at the darkness
then looks back at me

a stick goes over the falls at sunset

silence   the wind in the mirror

a lone duck
into one wave and out another
the autumn sea

the windy stars—
the distant gas station lights
go out

dead end—
a few leaves circle
in the headlights

late autumn
the billboard's shadow leans
into the woods

November evening—
the wind from a passing truck
ripples a roadside puddle

melting snow
the sun shines into the back
of an empty truck

LEQUITA VANCE

crescent moon
over the satellite dish
both face autumn

this heavy fog
no morning
no evening

GARY VAUGHN

circling a quiet pool water striders

ANITA VIRGIL

my spade turns
the dark earth   lets in
some sun

deep blue autumn sky;
from the cellar
a cricket sings

following me
deeper into my quilt
the wren's song

on the lowest shelf
jars full of
autumn sunlight

almost (down the path
        in the pouring rain) alone
box turtle

no sound to this
spring rain—
but the rocks darken

glittering heat—
the finches argue & argue
the viburnum droops

this spider web
    so different I
leave it alone

NICK VIRGILIO

another autumn
still silent in his closet:
father's violin

beyond the old pond,
the windows of the condo
mirror the autumn moon

Viet Nam Monument
darkened by the autumn rain:
my dead brother's name.

Autumn twilight:
the wreath on the door
lifts in the wind.

down from the stone bridge,
alone in the cold darkness:
the star in the creek

on the frozen snow
reflecting the rising sun:
the eyes of the dead doe

hospital quiet
I enter alone at twilight:
the scent of lilacs

on the creek bottom,
century-old snapping turtle:
years of beer bottles

over spatterdocks,
turning at corners of air:
dragonfly

In the empty church
at nightfall, a lone firefly
deepens the silence

Lily:
out of the water . . .
out of itself.

CAROL WAINRIGHT

killing frost—
I open the window
on silence

deer startled by the wind
the snowman
        alone again

cold drizzle—
even the duck
shaking it off

Listening
Only moonlight falls
on my shadow

After the foghorn
silence
drifts toward shore

spring
all day and all night
the frogs

PHYLLIS WALSH

blue damselfly
      rides a grass tip
            to water

MICHAEL DYLAN WELCH

gathering dawn—
   the first light
      filling the poppies

apple blossoms . . .
   into the wind
      spring rain

alone again
with its dragonfly
the puddle

summer heat—
   two squirrels
      meet on a wire

indian summer
   missing
the smell of rain

harvest moon—
the white spot
on the black cat

MARK ARVID WHITE

Glacier Bay—
into the cold stillness
the humpback's tail

NINA A. WICKER

partly cloudy—
a yellow cat taking her time
through the cemetery

Winter clouds
neck-deep in snow
an old gourd

the scent of cereus
again and again a moth
tries the screen

PAUL O. WILLIAMS

a cat watches me
across the still pond,
across our difference

only the fog
   or something beyond?
      the fog's shadow . . .

in the graveyard pine
   the quiet knock, knock
      of the woodpecker

Holsteins grazing
   in the summer rain—
      their tails switch slowly

a warm fall day,
learning from this rock
to do nothing

wind fills the air
  with this year's leaves—
    all perfect leaves

the cat deciding
  between the dark umbrella
  and the dark rain

ROD WILLMOT

a moth comes
to the evening primrose:
alone, yet not alone

paddling slowly
through the reeds
that touch her hair

the water stills:
a crayfish enters
the hollows of my face

half-moon through mist . . .
i lean now
on my axe

        headstand:
    a moth flutters past
my ankles

JOHN WILLS

unless you have fish
the pelican has no use
for you

the hills
release the summer clouds
one   by one   by one

touch of dawn
the snail withdraws
its horns

dusk   from rock to rock a waterthrush

an old field
throbbing with insects
the summer moon

the crawfish and i
wait for the water
to clear

goldenrod . . .
and in the distance
mountains

abandoned barn . . .
the faintest neighing
of horses

about
the white chrysanthemums
dusk comes early

winter mountains . . .
an old friend disappears
into the mist

nothing moves
in the snowy woods . . .
the cold!

far out
a lone duck bobs and bobs . . .
the lake in winter

VALORIE WOERDEHOFF

in morning fog
the white thistle
        blooming

late summer
    . . . walking
into our shadows

RUTH YARROW

turtle:
   her shell heaves
      through flickering grass

possum in the headlights
shakes her head
slowly

train platform:
each wet leaf
     face down

snowfall—
down the gorge the whitewater
         darkens

RICH YOUMANS

on the dark side of the fence
I rest
with the white camellia

winter rain . . .
snow geese flying over
the factory whistle

in the cellar
unglazed white pots
soaking moonlight

DONATELLA YOUNG

Alone
the Canada goose
scans the river

Early morning fog
on the backs of waves—
broken seawall

VIRGINIA BRADY YOUNG

Frog's shadow
    reaches the rock
    before the frog.

Blackbird and nightfall sharing the darkness

moonlight—
    a sand dune
    shifts

all my life
the silence
of the sun

white lilacs
before sunrise
their own light

PETER YOVU

low sun
my shadow crossing pebbles
and their shadows

cool morning
colors slide
up and down the spider thread

JOHN ZIEMBA

in my loneliness
I let the persimmon
get overripe

Winter—
throwing a stone into the waves . . .
nothing.

In the back alley,
one light . . .
the old snow

ARIZONA ZIPPER

Right in the middle
of the cat's yawn—
a pink tongue

a blossom falls
one by one
the peepers begin

Opening its eyes
closing its eyes
a cat in the sun

falling asleep;
the moon
is still there

ROBERT H. ZUKOWSKI

April rain—
the name   almost smooth
with the tombstone

ABBREVIATIONS

The following abbreviations have been used in the credits:

A *The Alchemist*

AH *An Anthology of Haiku by the People of the United States and Canada* (JAL 1988)

aa *the ant's afternoon, Haiku and senryu from members of the Boston Haiku Society,* ed. Raffael de Gruttola, Lawrence Rungren & John Ziemba (Aether Press, 1990)

BSM *Beneath A Single Moon, Buddhism in Contemporary American Poetry,* ed. Kent Johnson & Craig Paulenich (Shambhala, 1991)

BS *Brussels Sprout*

C *Cicada*

D *Dragonfly*

EH *Erotic Haiku,* ed. Rod Willmot (Black Moss Press, 1983)

F *Frogpond*

HA *The Haiku Anthology,* ed. Cor van den Heuvel (Simon & Schuster, 1986)

HCH *Haiku Canada 15th Anniversary Holograph Anthology 1992*

HCN *Haiku Canada Newsletter*

HCS *Haiku Canada Sheet*

HCC *HAIKU, Canadian Anthology,* ed. Dorothy Howard & André Duhaime (éditions Asticou, 1985)

HI *Haiku International*

HJ *Haiku Journal, Yuki Teikei Haiku Society Members' Anthology 1990-1991*

HQ *Haiku Quarterly*

HSA *Haiku Society of America Newsletter*

hnh *haru no hana haiku* (Haiku Poets of Upstate New York, 1992)

I *Inkstone*

K *Ko*

LSR *The Land of Seven Realms, Haiku Writers of Gualala Arts,* ed. Jane Reichhold (AHA Books, 1989)

MDN *Mainichi Daily News*

MGH *Milkweed, A Gathering of Haiku,* ed. Marshall Hryciuk (Nietzche's Brolly, 1987)

M *Mirrors*

MH *Modern Haiku*

NC *New Cicada*

op *old pond*

PT *Persimmon Tree*

PNE *Pine Needles*

PN *Poetry Nippon*

PJL *Point Judith Light*

PB *A Poppy Blooms,* ed. Patricia Donegan (Two Autumns Press, 1991)

RP *The Red Pagoda*

T *Tidepool*

un. unpublished

VI *Virtual Image*

WC *Wind Chimes*

W *Woodnotes*

PERMISSIONS

The editor has made every attempt to contact the author or copyright holder of the haiku in this volume and would appreciate hearing from any author or copyright holder not so contacted.

Bernard M. Aaronson: "From every side" and "The crows unseen" from MH XX:1(89); "It also rained" from F XII:2(89); by permission of Pat Aaronson.

Suezan Aikins: "Whirling snowflakes" from D 15:1(89); "sleeting dawn" from F XII 1(89); "whistling wind" from MH XIX:1(88); by permission of the author.

Ann Atwood: "Summer is over" from F VIII:4(85); "Twilight growing" from F IX: 3(86); "Finally" from F XII:3(89); "how visible" from MH XIX:3(88); by permission of the author.

Nick Avis: "waking from a dream" from MH XIII:2(82); "november nightfall" from HCC; "the telephone" from MH XV:3(84); "stepping from stone to stone" from MH XVI:2(85); "deep inside" from F XI:4(88); "midday heat" from F XIII:3(90); "remembering the lie" and "reading her letter" from *you aim to love* (Burnt Lake Press, 1988); "we say we're sorry" from F X:1(87); "night curtain" from MH XV:2(84); by permission of the author.

Winona Baker: The three haiku are from *MOSS-HUNG TREES, Haiku of the West Coast* (REFLECTIONS Publisher, 1992); by permission of REFLECTIONS Publisher and the author.

Francine Banwarth: "a circle of light" from BS VII:1(90); "in cellar darkness" is un.; by permission of the author.

Herb Barrett: Both haiku are from "Moving Away" HCS 1985-86; by permission of the author.

M. L. Bittle-DeLapa: "starting to rain" from hnh; "paling twilight" from F IX: 1(86); "firefly there" from W 6(91); by permission of the author.

Tom Blessing: "the doe" from F XIII:2(90).

Marianne Bluger: "rain-rinsed twilight" from "The Marigolds" HCS 1988-89; "flat tire" and "ah   these soft spring nights" from "April &" HCS 1985-86; "cloudy afternoon" from F XIII:4(90); "with what enviable" from HCH; "buzzing with flies" from D 15:1(89); "utterly still" from MGH; "twisted old lilacs" from NC 2:1(85); by permission of the author.

Bob Boldman: "locking the door" from F IX:1(86); "distant lightening" from MH XV:2(84); "composing me" from WC 4(82); "whatever I wanted" from F IX:3(86); "dawn" and "dark" from BSM; "utterly still" from WC 17(85); by permission of the author.

John Brandi: "a frog too" from *Poems from the Green Parade* (Tooth of Time Books, 1990); "After the argument" from *Circling* (Exiled-In-America Press, 1988); The remaining four haiku are from *Weeding the Cosmos* (You-Hoo Press, 1991); by permission of the author.

Chuck Brickley: "a car" and "the ledger blurs" from MH XIII:3(82); "sheet lightning" and "the crow" from MH XIV:1(83); by permission of the author.

Beatrice Brissman: "The way silence waits" from MH XX:2(89); by permission of the author.

Naomi Y. Brown: "red ants zig-zag" from MH XXI:2(90); "dusk settles" from MH XXIII:2(92); by permission of the author.

C. M. Buckaway: "July afternoon" from MGH; "Tinkling brook" from "Tinkling Brook" HCS 1985-86; "The autumn moon shines" from NC 4:1(87); "Among the poplars" from F XI:3(88); "Closing my eyelids" from F XI:4(88); "Alone at dusk" from F XII:2(89); by permission of the author.

Margaret Chula: All four haiku are un.; by permission of the author.

Tom Clausen: "downpour" from F XIV:2(91); "daybreak frost" from MH XXIII:2(92); by permission of the author.

Denise Coney: "after the storm" from HCC; "full moon" from "Swallowtail" HCS 1987-88; "second snowfall" from WC 15(85); "yellow on yellow" from MGH; by permission of the author.

Steve Dalachinsky: "spring" from F XI:2(88); by permission of the author.

L. A. Davidson: "such a twittering," "in a blizzard," and "crossing the table" from *The Shape of the Tree* (Wind Chimes, 1982); "on the roof" from F XI:4(88); "through a closed motel window" from F VII:3(84); "Monday morning" from F XIV:4(91); "snow predicted" from WC 4(82); "What to say?" from NC 4:1(87); "on shore alone" from F XIV:3(91); by permission of the author.

Raffael de Gruttola: "in the house plants" from BS IX:2(92); "touched by the moon" and "floating up river" from "Prism" HCS 1987-88; "endless day" from BS VI:2(89); "after some silence" from W 5(90); by permission of the author.

Charles Dickson: "young trout lilies" and "abandoned pasture" from MH XXI:2(90); "marsh twilight" from NC 6:2(89); "mountain pool" from MH XXII:3(91); "standing on one foot" from W 4(90); "migrating geese" from MH XX:1(89); "sagging footbridge" and "dense fog" from "Appalachian Twilight" HCS 1986-87; "field of Queen Anne's lace" from F XI:2(88); "splash of wild plums" from MH XIX:1(88); "September gust" from K (87); "twilight storm" from K (89); "winter beach" from W 7(90); "out of the fog bank" from BS VI:2(89); by permission of Virginia P. Dickson.

315

Mike Dillon: "October hot spell" from MH XIX:1(88); "Parked bulldozer" from MH XXII:3(91); "Winter rain" from MH XXII:2(91); by permission of the author.

Patricia Donegan: "I lay down," "Last night," and "People are gone" from *Without Warning* (Parallax Press, 1990); "Tonight" is un.; by permission of the author.

Betty Drevniok: "Lilac scent," "Someone calls," and "Spring snow" from MGH; "Morning coffee" from MH XIII:2(82); "Full moon at midnight" from "Smell of Earth" HCS 1986-87; by permission of the author.

Michael Dudley: "lulling me to sleep" from *through the green fuse* (High/Coo Press, 1983); "oaring" from *A Man in a Motel Room* (High/Coo Press, 1986); by permission of the author.

Virginia Egermeier: "Same old road" from F X:4(87); "Spring thaw" from D 15: 1(89); by permission of the author.

Bernard Lionel Einbond: "frog pond" from AH; "the thousand colors" is un.; by permission of the author.

Lesley Einer: "before the quail" from HJ; "holding" from F XVI:1(91); by permission of the author.

David Elliott: "a blue heron," "Dark so soon," "Some year," and "October sunset" from *Wind in the Trees* (AHA Books, 1992); "a spider climbs" from F XI:1(88); "Below zero" from MH XIX:1(88); "The silence after" from F XI:4(88); "Hard to be" and "Among leafless trees" from PJL I:1(92); "Spring thaw" from F XIII:2 (90); "4 a.m." from F XII:2(89); "Such lightness" from F XIV:1(91); by permission of the author.

Margarita Mondrus Engle: "drifting fog" and "rush hour" from F XIII:4(90); "old orchard" from F XI:4(88); "afternoon sun" from F XIII:3(90); "dusk" from D 15:1(89); "autumn night" from F XII:4(89); by permission of the author.

Ruth Eshbaugh: "cold moon" from I 3:4(87).

Sister Mary Thomas Eulberg: "only that star" from F V:2(82); "through window frames" from F IX:4(86); "no need" and "fresh snow" from F X:4(87); "everything's strange" from MH XX:2(89); by permission of the author.

Dee Evetts: "Within" from MH XIX:1(88); "willows turn" and "the river" from *A Small Ceremony* (From Here Press, 1988); by permission of the author.

Liz Fenn: "First day of spring" from MH XX:2(89); by permission of the author.

Ross Figgins: "autumn shadows" and "twilit pasture" from MH XVIII:3(87); by permission of the author.

Sarah Fitzjarrald: "so still" from MH XXII:2(91); by permission of the author.

Ellen Florman: "Midwinter night" from F XIV:4(91); "A cold moon" from F XIV:2(91); by permission of the author.

Sylvia Forges-Ryan: "sparrow chirping" from F VIII:1(85); "January coldness" and "snowdrifts" from NC 3:2(86); by permission of the author.

Marie Forsyth: "quiet pond" from D 15:4(91); by permission of the author.

Marco Fraticelli: "Outside the cemetery" from "Funeral Sequence" HCS 1985-86; "The old man" and "Morning train" from *Night Coach* (Guernica Editions, 1983); by permission of the author.

Sandra Fuhringer: "the open grave" from I 1:3(82); "Autumn wind" from HCC; "Moonless night" from MGH; "one autumn cricket" from WC 6(82); "Straight down" from F V:2(82); "rain all day" from WC 7 (83); "alone on the lake" from WC 9(83); by permission of the author.

Frederick Gasser: "Yard sale" from D 15:1(89); "late evening" from D 15:2(89); "abandoned sidewalk" from F X:3(87); by permission of the author.

Bob Gates: "winter burial" from F XI:1(88); by permission of the author.

Larry Gates: "a cloud on the water" and "a quiet afternoon" from F XI:3(88); by permission of the author.

Garry Gay: "September stillness" from MH XXI:3(90); "Early morning frost" and "Seal voices" from PB; "3:15 am" from WC 4(82); "Hiking" from F XII:3(89); "Her mailbox" from F XIII:3(90); "The yellow lily" from *The Silent Garden* (Smythe-Waithe Press, 1982); "Last summer moon" is un.; by permission of the author.

Robert Gibson: "Beyond the lawn" and "The autumn moon" from HJ; "Sunrise" is un.; by permission of the author.

Barry Goodmann: "teasing the crab" from F XII:3(89); by permission of the author.

LeRoy Gorman: "nitefall" from I 3:1(85); "first snow" from MH XIV:2(83); "rainpuddles" and "a brown leaf" from *Heart's Garden* (Guernica Editions, 1983); "in the hills" from MH XXIII:2(92); "cool wind" from A III:2(86); by permission of the author.

Larry Gross: "cicadas stop" from PNE II:1(89); "dangling" from D 15:2(89); "the still air" from HQ III:1(91); "by firelight" from PJL I:1(92); by permission of the author.

Lee Gurga: "first spring day" from NC 5:2(89); "hillside of troutlily" from MH XIX:3(88); "trying the old pump" from MH XIX:1(88); "each waiting" from NC 6:2 (89); "spot of sunlight" from *The Measure of Emptiness* (Press Here, 1991); "going out of my way" from F XI:4(88); by permission of the author.

Rosamond Haas: "from pondview bridge" from MH XIX:3(88); by permission of the author.

317

318

Foster Jewell: "Still there," "Not hearing the silence," and "Last raindrop" from WC 5(82).

Randy Johnson: "slower than the rest" from F X:1(87); "melting into the night" from F X:4(873; by permission of the author.

Robert N. Johnson: "the dark hawk" from F X:4(87); "winter cottonwoods" from F XII:1(89); by permission of the author.

Jean Jorgensen: "afternoon hush" from MH XXII:3(91); by permission of the author.

Jim Kacian: "the door slams" from PN X:5(91); "heat lightning" from I 5:1(91); "plum blossoms" from MH XXI:2(90); "summer wind" from HJ; by permission of the author.

Leroy Kanterman: "Sunset" from F XIII:3(90); by permission of the author.

Adele Kenny: "moonrise" from F XIII:2(90); "winter solstice" from MH XV:2(84); "on the wet street" from F VI:4(83); "sleepless night" from W 6(90); by permission of the author.

Michael Ketchek: "ten minutes to five" from MH XXII:2(91); "light morning mist" from MH XIX:3(88); "waves crash" from F XV:1(92); by permission of the author.

Jerry Kilbride: "christmas night" from F IX:4(86); "northern lights" from MH XIV: 1(83); "mother lode country" from F XIII:3(90); by permission of the author.

George Klacsanzky: All three haiku are un.; by permission of the author.

Elsie Kolashinski: "already the bees" from F XV:1(92); "dry creek bed" from MH XXIII:2(92); by permission of the author.

Elizabeth Searle Lamb: "a white horse" from HCH; "the old irrigation ditch," "in morning sun," "field of white iris," "before firstlight," and "in the last light" from *Casting into a Cloud: Southwest Haiku* (From Here Press, 1985); "for this one moment" from MH XXII:3(91); "the elk herd" from MH XVIII:3(87); "early blizzard" from MH XXII:1(91); "and after" from EH; by permission of the author.

Jane K. Lambert: "Summer shower" from D 15:3(89); by permission of the author.

David E. LeCount: "last night's soft rain" and "turtle skeleton" from F VI:3(83); "dusk dimming" from F XIII:3(90); by permission of the author.

Kenneth C. Leibman: "November morning," "no breeze," and "sunflowers" from *alachua: North Florida Haiku* (Druidoaks, 1990); "cow pasture" from D 15:2(89); by permission of the author.

Minna Lerman: "The way the breeze" from W 1(91); "barren maple" from HSA (Oct. 23, 1989); the remaining five haiku are un.; by permission of the author.

319

Leatrice Lifshitz: "my tracks" and "without a breeze" from F XII:2(89); "snowstorm" from F XIII:1(90); "winter thaw" from MH XXI:2(90); "glass doors" from MH XXII:1(91); "nameless" from D 15:3(89); by permission of the author.

Rebecca Lilly: "Spring clouds" and "Where I spotted the deer" from F XV:1(92); "Evening rain" from MH XXIII:2(92); by permission of the author.

Geraldine C. Little: "frosted sedge grass" from F VI:4(83); "coming home" from F VII:2(84); "how delicately" from MH XX:2(89); "winter solstice" from F XII: 1(89); "Full winter moon" from MH XIV:1(83); "on the bank" from K(90); "The bright silence" from F V:3(82); "Listening" from F X:3(87); "in the polished doorknob" from *Star-Mapped* (Silver Apples Press, 1989); "summer afternoon" from F VIII:3(85); "Eaves" from F X:3(87); by permission of the author.

Matthew Louvière: "Moonlit night" from F XIV:3(91); "These chrysanthemums" and "The goose" from K(87); "The white cat," "Winter fog," and "Spring wind" from K(89); "Winter wind" from D 14:7(87); "Dark shadow" from MH XXII:2(91); "A mule" from K(91); "Twilight" from I 3:4(87); "White butterfly" from NC 7:1(91); "Thunder" from MH XX:2(89); "Heavy summer air" from MH XIX:3(88); "One dragonfly" from MH XXI:3(90); by permission of the author.

Peggy Lyles: "nip of fall" from F X:3(87); "first frost" from MH XVIII:3(87); "Tea fragrance" from MH XIII:2(82); by permission of the author.

Tom Lynch: "almost asleep" and "suddenly here" from *Rain Drips from the Trees: Haibun along the trans-Canadian Highway* (English Department, Holy Names College, Oakland, CA); by permission of the author.

Barbara McCoy: "a few red tomatoes" from F V:1(82); "autumn sunset" from NC 4:1 (87); "January cold" from F VIII:1(85), "Snow beyond the pane" from WC 12(84); by permission of the author.

anne mckay: "in the april orchard" from K(89); "from her window" from MH XXII:2 (91); by permission of the author.

Dorothy McLaughlin: "alone in the rain" from F XIII:4(90); "drifts of snow" from F XII:4(89); "apple orchard" from D 14:1(85-86); "no stars" from D 15:4(91); by permission of the author.

Donald McLeod: "barnacles" and "momentary dolphins" from F X:3(87); by permission of the author.

Michael McNierney: "the boat's horn" from F X:2(87); "wolf spider" from F X:4 (87); by permission of the author.

Carol Montgomery: "middle of the highway" from I 4:4(91); "autumn storm" from F IX:4(86); "in my silver" from F XIV:1(91); "between pinches" from I 5:2(92); by permission of the author.

Lenard D. Moore: "twilight mist" from NC 2:1(85); "winter river," "in the moonlit breeze," "moon dusk," "evening mist," and "Long after sundown" from *the open eye* (The North Carolina Haiku Society Press, 1986); "a moth rises" from K(87); "plum-scented farm" from I 3:3(87); "abandoned mill" from MH XXI:3(90); "hill after hill" from MH XXII:1(91); by permission of the author.

June Moreau: "it's a wonder" and "sunrise" from F XIV:2(91); "the sky's" from W 7(90); "Clumps of cranberry" from MH XXIII:2(92); "squinting my eyes" from MH XXII:3(91); "shaping itself" from aa; "a hornet" from W 6(90); by permission of the author.

Marlene Mountain: "thrush song" from MH XXI:3(90); "beyond the sink" from MH XX:2(89); "a hot day" from F X:3(87); "autumn dusk" and "cloudy day" from F IX:4 (86); "faded flowers" from HA; by permission of the author.

Charles D. Nethaway, Jr.: "waterfall at night" from F V:4(82); "spring" from F VIII:1(85); "monarch" from MH XX:1(89); "late summer" from D 15:2(89); by permission of the author.

Patricia Neubauer: "down this old lane" from BS IX:2(92); "hesitating" from F XI:2(88); "dusk" from F XIV:3(91); "black ant" from MH XXII:2(91); by permission of the author.

Patricia Niehoff: "as I approach" from D 14:7(87); "reaching into" from I 3:4(87); by permission of the author.

Joe Nutt: "new leaves" from MH XX:2(89); "the squirrel's tail" from M 3:2(90); "silence," "sunrise," "in the yellow sun," "tent caterpillars," "after the bellow," "early frost," and "the dugs" from *Kernels* (Nutt Studio, 1989); "another parting" from BS VI:2(89); "Flickering" from MH XVIII:2(87); by permission of the author.

Brent Partridge: "cooper's hawk" from I 5:1(91); "hard rain" from W 9(91); "autumn wind" from MH XXII:1(91); "preceding me" from F XII:3(89); "autumn fog" from F XIII:4(90); "i carry a cricket" from BS VIII:1(91); "no two falling" from MH XIX:3(88); "the rest of" from MH XXII:2(91); "checking the breeze" from F XIV:3(91); "down into" from BS IX:2(92); by permission of the author.

Bill Pauly: "tonight your face" from F XI:1(88); "white undersides" from EH; "seventh day" from F IX:4(86); by permission of the author.

Brett Peruzzi: "Reflected" from F X:4(87); "dilapidated cottage" from F XIV:2 (91); by permission of the author.

Alan Pizzarelli: "cold wind" from F VII:3(84); "the ferris wheel" and "the windowpane" from *The Flea Circus* (423 Berkeley Ave., Bloomfield, NJ, 1989); "in the stream," "bitter cold," "twilight," and "in front of the go-go bar" from *City Beat* (423 Berkeley Ave., Bloomfield, NJ, 1991); "the shade springs" and "on the merry-go-round" from HA; "nightfall" and "light rain" from MH XX:2 (89); by permission of the author.

Francine Porad: "crab" from F XII:4(89); "drone" from NC 6:1(89); "night clouds" from F XIV:l(91); "side by side" from T 8(91); "twilight deepens" from T 6(89); by permission of the author.

Claire Pratt: "clean summer breeze," "O forsythia," and "October mist" from "Dog Days" HCS 1986-87; "starless night" from I 1:1(82); "darkened branch" from MGH; by permission of the author.

David Priebe: "Autumn cloud" from PB; "On a steppingstone" from D 15:3(89); "In shallow water" from F XII:3(89); by permission of the author.

Gloria H. Procsal: "from winter sky" from F X:1(87); "april sunshine" from F X:2 (87); "out of the rainy hills" from MH XXI:3(90); by permission of the author.

Viola Provenzano: "river fog" from MH XIX:3(88); "empty moonlit beach" from D 4:2(82); "cedar grove" from MH XX:1(89); by permission of the author.

Anthony J. Pupello: "winter chill" from F XIV:4(91); "shadows on the wall" from MH XVIII:3(87); by permission of the author.

Frederick A. Raborg, Jr.: "in the frigid wind" from F VIII:1(85); by permission of the author.

Zhanna P. Rader: "Frozen moon" from BS VI:2(89); "Blue mud dauber" from MH XX:2 (89); "Stepping" from D 14:7(87); "All at once" from F X:3(87); by permission of the author.

George Ralph: "from the shadows" and "chilly night" from F X:3(87); "a patch of sunlight" from F XII:2(89); "midday blizzard" from D 14:7(87); "ice-encrusted" from D 15:2(89); by permission of the author.

Jane Reichhold: "in the dark" from "A Tale Without a Mouse" HCS 1986-87; "a barking dog," "such a storm," and "winter" from *As Stones Cry Out* (Humidity Productions, 1987); "evening fog," "autumn wind," and "sea lions bark" from *A Dictionary of Haiku* (AHA Books, 1992); "how snugly" from *Thumbtacks on a Calendar* (Humidity Productions, 1984); "October sun" and "New Year's Day" from *Tigers in a Teacup, Collected Haiku* (AHA Books, 1988); by permission of the author.

Werner Reichhold: "tidepool" from LSR; "fiddler crab" and "desert" from *Tidalwave* (AHA Books, 1989); by permission of the author.

Barbara Ressler: "Easter lily" from F XII:2(89); by permission of the author.

David Rice: "surfbirds" from MH XX:1(89); by permission of the author.

Lee Richmond: "Along this road" and "A speckled hen" from *Autumn Sleep* (189 Parsons Drive, Hempstead, NY, 1983); "Scolding myself," "In mother's voice," and "Before today" from *Roots in Winter* (189 Parsons Drive, Hempstead, NY, 1984); "Winter chrysanthemums" and "The loneliness" from

322

Diary of a Winter Fly (189 Parsons Drive, Hempstead, NY, 1982); "Without a place" and "A winter chrysanthemum" from *Fireflies* (Black Swan Books, 1989); by permission of John Walsh.

Andy Roberts: "salamander" from MH XXI:3(90); by permission of the author.

Frank K. Robinson: "drifting clouds" from MH XIX:3(88); "through the dark" from MH XX:1(89); "mountain stillness" from MH XXII:1(91); "indian summer" from F XII:3(89); "sleepless night" is un.; "a gentle tugging" from MH XVIII:2(87); "across the road" from MH XIX:1(88); "autumn moon" from MH XVIII:3(87); "so many years" and "fog lifting" from MH XV:2(84); "first flashes" from F VII:4 (84); "chrysanthemums" from F VI:1(83); "still white world" from MH XVIII:3 (87); "a sparrow searches" from MH XV:3(84); by permission of the author.

Emily Romano: "scrawny rabbit" from MH XV:3(84); "through thinning mist" from MH XVIII:3(87); "chilly morning" from MH XXI:2(90); "Indian summer" from MH XXI:3(90); "quiet waters" from D 15:2(89); "dusk" from MH XIX:1(88); by permission of the author.

Ronan: "sea gulls placing" from BS IX:2(92); by permission of the author.

Mildred A. Rose: "Sun moves" and "Sparrows twittering" from "Still Life" HCS 1986-87; by permission of Don Rose.

Raymond Roseliep: "piano practice" from VI 1:1(82) copyright © W. Elliot Grieg 1982, copyright © Daniel J. Rogers 1983; "seance" and "footbridge" from *Rabbit in the Moon* (Alembic Press, 1983), copyright © Raymond Roseliep 1983 and renewed 1985, Daniel J. Rogers; by permission of Daniel J. Rogers.

Bruce Ross: "abandoned house" is un.; "luminous moonlight" from *The Trees* (The Plowman, 1991); "still spring night" from hnh; "a spider huddled" from PN X:5 (91); "spring chill" and "faint spring mist" from MH XXIII:3(92); "morning silence" from NC 8:2(91); "loon's cry" from D 15:3(89); "early autumn sun" from HI 3(92); "the gray squirrel pair," "migrating monarchs," and "a milk-white spider" from *thousands of wet stones* (M.A.F. Press, 1988); "autumn drizzle" and "a leaping squirrel" from NC 8:1(91); "early morning woods" from MH XXIV:1(83); "puzzled crow's" and "under the mallard's" from M 3:2(90); "frozen Quaker pond" from MH XXIII:2(92); by permission of the author.

Alexis Rotella: "At the top" from MH XIII:1(82); "soaking up the moon," "Lightning," "A wet spot," and "After the first snow" from BSM; "The silence" from MH XVI:2(85); "swans" and "Not speaking" from HA; "Among morning-glories" from I 2:3(84); "An old woman" and "Up through the moon" from F XV:1(92); "Picking the daisy" from MH XX:3(89); "I let it pass" from K(91); "bulging" from F IX:2(86); "Wild phlox" from K(88); "One little woodpecker" from "Star Power" HCS 1990-91; "a swallowtail" from F XI:3(88); "Does that one star" from BS VIII:1(91); "dusk" from MH XV:2(84); "The gull" from K(87); "I forgot why" from MH XIV:2(82); "winter chill" from MH XIV:2(83); "Autumn stillness" from MH XXI:2(90); "Still on its vine" from MH XX:2(89); "autumn sky" from F VII:2(84); by permission of the author.

Hal Roth: "sparrow" from F V:1(82); "lifting the hay bale" from F VIII:2(84); "only a shanty" from BS II:4(82); "night" from HI 2(91); by permission of the author.

Lawrence Rungren: "kept awake" from F VIII:2(85); "the cat hisses" from D 10:15 (89); "autumn comes" from F XII:4(89); "November dusk" from MH XX:1(89); by permission of the author.

Rebecca Rust: "Overnight snow" from F VIII:4(85); "in moonlit sea" from F IX:3(86); "dark rainy street" from K(91); "night swamp" from F XII:2(89); by permission of the author.

Miriam Sagan: "The whole neighborhood" and "Wanted to buy" from I 3:4(87); "Unseen at first" from MH XVIII:3(87); by permission of the author.

Lewis Sanders: "Without frog sounds" from RP V:1(88); "Winter rain" from "Another Winter Chill" HCS 1987-88; "Snow predicted" from BS VI:2(89); by permission of the author.

Steve Sanfield: "So silent," "Summer mountains," "Without a moon," "No fire," "The naked trees," and "Loons cry" from *A New Way* (Tooth of Time Books, 1983); "The loudest sound" from *He Smiled to Himself* (Shakti Press, 1990); by permission of the author.

Margaret Saunders: "Through" from *Snapdragons!* (South Western Ontario Poetry, 1982); "Winter stillness" from T 3(86); by permission of the author.

Grant Savage: "October evening" and "Look!!" from "Hummingbird Dew-drops" HCS 1987-88; "Softly" and "After the storm" are un.; by permission of the author.

Sharon Lee Shafii: "Cold wind" from D 15:4(91); "outdoor cafe" from D 15:1(89); "Frozen dawn" from I 4:3(90); "Pileated woodpecker" from D 15:4(91); "after the storm" from F XIV:1(91); by permission of the author.

Eileen Sherry: "snow dusted branches" from MH XXI:3(90); by permission of the author.

Helen J. Sherry: "caught between" from D 14:7(87); "cold wind" from D 15:1(89); "daybreak" and "ebb tide" from *Colors of Haiku* (Chōchō Books, 1991); by permission of the author.

Rob Simbeck: "full moon" from F XII:3(89); by permission of the author.

Stephen Small: "I did nothing" from aa; by permission of the author.

Dorothy Cameron Smith: "even the clouds" from T 8(91); "November fog" from "Hummingbirds" HCS 1986-87; by permission of Kent Smith.

Margaret R. Smith: "as if they owned" from MH XVIII:3(87); "trapped" from MH XXI:3(90); by permission of the author.

Tom Smith: "new year's sun," "hummingbird," and "rainfall" from *The Broken Iris* (Persephone Press, 1990); by permission of the author.

Karen Sohne: "not knowing" from WC 22(88); "looking straight" from WC 19(87); "above its nearly still" from F X:2(87); "such red tulips" from F XI:2(88); "no moonlight" from F XIV:1(91); "rain" from F XI:4(88); "walking in winter" from F X:1(87); by permission of the author.

Keith Southward: "Bulrushes explode" and "In the fading light" from MGH; by permission of the author.

Robert Spiess: "a spring breeze rises," "Asparagus bed," "Evening clouds," "A dirt road," "Becoming dusk," "First light," "A breeze on the stream," "Summer is turning," and "Winter wind" from *The Shape of Water* (Modern Haiku Press, 1982); "a round melon," "an unspoken love," "canoeing the bend," and "the field's evening fog" from *The Cottage of Wild Plum* (Modern Haiku Press, 1991); by permission of the author.

Ruby Spriggs: "within closing petals" and "on one leg" from "inthelakeinme" HCS 1985-86; "rain in the night" from D 15:4(91); the remaining seven haiku are from *Sun Shadow, Moon Shadow* (Heron Cove Press, 1986); by permission of the author.

Elizabeth St Jacques: "dodging" from F XIII:3(90); "mallard feather" from W 7(90); "march winds" from C V:3(91); "lightning flash" from W 10(91); "the cave's mouth" from BS VII:2(90); "swaying" from C V:2(90); "in the night barn" from NC 6:2(89); "on a step" from I 4:3(90); by permission of the author.

Ebba Story: "first light" from F XIV:4(91); "gleaming gold" from F XV:1(92); by permission of the author.

Richard Straw: "black horses" from F XI:4(88); by permission of the author.

Denver Stull: "winter ice storm" from F XI:1(88); by permission of the author.

Christopher Suarez: "old warehouse" from F X:1(87); by permission of the author.

Dave Sutter: "Summer storm" from F XIII:3(90); "Among the reeds" from PB; "Summer mountain" from MH XXIII:2(92); by permission of the author.

George Swede: "Falling pine needles" from HCN V:3(90); "Into the mailbox" from I 2:1(83); "Dropping stone after stone" and "Lightning flash" from *High Wire Spider* (Three Trees Press, 1986); "After the rain" from I 1:1(82); "dusk" from F XIII:4(90); "Divorce proceedings" from I 2:4(85); "Lilac-scented breeze" from MH XV:3(84); "Circling higher" from F X:3(87); "Dawn" from PN VII:1&2(83); "Night begins" from EH; "Broken mirror" from MH XIX:1(88); by permission of the author.

Wally Swist: "walking farther into" from MH XIX:3(88); "we wake at dawn" and "at the edge" from *Unmarked Stones* (Burnt Lake Press, 1988); "opened so boldly" from F XV:1(92); "spring night" from MH XX:3(89); "in the one unbroken" from F XII:3(89); "stopping in my steps" from F X:4(87); "opening into forest" from F XIX:2(91); "Indian summer" from RP V:2(88); "deep bend of the brook" from MH XXII:3(91); "sun burns off" from MH XIX:1(88); "beside the brook's rush" and "lingering" from F XI:4(88); "startled from the thicket" from F XIII:2(90); "foggy morning" from MH XXII:1(90); "standing out" from HQ II:3(90); "Pausing to listen" from MH XXII:2(91); "new moon" from MH XX:1(89); "the insistent voice" from F XIII:1(90); "new snow" from F XII:1(89); "plummeting" from MH XXIII:2(92); by permission of the author.

Kenneth Tanemura: "a single rose" and "sleepless" are un.; "the lightning flashes" from MH XXI:1(91); "only the stone-smell" from BS IX:1(92); "a starry night" from MH XX:3(89); "a corner" from MH XXI:3(90); by permission of the author.

K. G. Teal: Both haiku are from F XI:4(88); by permission of the author.

Richard Thompson: Both haiku are from F XV:1(92); by permission of the author.

Richard Tice: "a day at the office" from D 15:3(89); "bare trees" from D 15:4(91); by permission of the author.

Tom Tico: "Sandpipers" from D 14:7(87); "a windless morning" from I 2:2(84); "Beneath darkening skies" from PT I:2(90); "Dusk" from D 15:3(89); "Engulfing" from MH XIX:3(88); "a morning of fog" from W 6(90); "on every step" from MH XX:2(89); by permission of the author.

Sue Stapleton Tkach: "Flooded by spring rain" from MH XX:2(89); "Sooner or later" from BS VI:2(89); by permission of the author.

vincent tripi: "Letting" from NC 7:1(90); "Persimmons" and "Another song" from NC 8:1(91); "Colouring itself" from F XIV:3(91); "Almost full moon" from F XIV:1(91); "Abandoned ferris wheel" from MH XX:2(89); "Without a trail" from F XIV:2(91); by permission of the author.

Anna Vakar: "still climbing" from NC 4:1(87); "in the large shadow" from F XI:4(88); "sunlight in the snow" from NC 5:2(88); by permission of the author.

Cor van den Heuvel: "arms folded," "three clothespins," "under the pier," "a lone duck," "the windy stars," and "melting snow" from MH XXII:1(91); "by the lawn's edge," "dead end," and "late autumn" from F XIV:1(91); "a stick goes over," "silence," and "November evening" from *Dark* (Chant Press, 1982); by permission of the author.

Lequita Vance: "crescent moon" from F XIII:4(90); "this heavy fog" from W 5(90); by permission of the author.

Donatella Young: "Alone" is un.; "early morning fog" from MH XXII:1(91); by permission of the author.

Virginia Brady Young: "Frog's shadow" from F VII:3(84); "Blackbird" from F VIII:1(85); "Moonlight" from F XIII:1(90); "all my life" from MH XXII:1(91); "white lilacs" from HCN V:1(89); by permission of the author.

Peter Yovu: "low sun" from F XIV:1(91); "cool morning" from MH XXII:1(91); by permission of the author.

John Ziemba: "in my loneliness" from aa; "Winter" from F XII:1(89); "in the back alley" from D 15:2(89); by permission of the author.

Arizona Zipper: "Right in the middle" from F VI:2(83); "a blossom falls" from F VIII:2(85); "Opening its eyes" from F XII:3(89); "falling asleep" from F VIII:1(85); by permission of the author.

Robert H. Zukowski: "April rain" from MH XXI:3(90); by permission of the author.

INDEX

330

About the Author

Bruce Ross is the author of three haiku collections and has published haiku and critical theory in journals throughout the U.S., Europe, and Japan. He is the 1995 president of the Haiku Society of America.